BETWEEN CHAPTERS

PRAISE FOR
BETWEEN CHAPTERS

"Zibby writes like a woman with her life cracked wide open—and the courage to look straight inside. *Between Chapters* is funny, tender, unflinching, and so deeply human. These essays meet us in the messy middle of becoming, where nothing is certain but everything is alive. If you've ever found yourself starting over, questioning everything, or scribbling your way through the chaos just to make sense of it, you will feel profoundly seen here. This book is a companion, a permission slip, and a reminder: It is never too late to rewrite your story."

—JEN HATMAKER, bestselling author of *Awake*

"It's wonderful! Intimate, frank, and familiar, *Between Chapters* is pure delight. Zibby parses the joys and pains of midlife awakening and reinvention in these bite-sized essays, each one landing with authenticity and humor and honesty."

—SUSAN ORLEAN, bestselling author of *The Library Book* and *Joyride*

"A reminder to us all that the messy middle of life is no joke! Disarmingly honest, funny, and a raw exploration of the choices we make and why we make them. Thank you for allowing us to dive in with you, Zibby."

—AMY GRIFFIN, founder of G9 Ventures and bestselling author of *The Tell*

"An inspiring story about reinvention, entrepreneurship, motherhood, and finding your people."

—BOBBI BROWN, founder of Jones Road Beauty and bestselling author of *Still Bobbi*

"I loved this book and read it in one sitting! Warm, funny, and deeply moving, *Between Chapters* captures the moment so many women reach in midlife when they realize the script they've been following no longer fits. With humor and honesty, it reminds us that starting over isn't failure; it's the beginning of the most authentic chapter yet."

—ELYCE ARONS, bestselling author of *We Might Just Make It After All*

"Delightful. This will resonate with so many women! A colorful pastiche of an unabashedly honest New York mom, proving we crystallize into our bravest and best selves in middle age, it's never too late for a career reboot, and the best is yet to come."

—JILL KARGMAN, creator of *Odd Mom Out* and bestselling author of *Sprinkle Glitter on My Grave*

"*Between Chapters* is filled with essays that are funny, moving, and wonderfully relatable. With her signature wit, Zibby reflects on the many roles that shape a life—mom, author, entrepreneur, wife, friend—and so many times, while reading, I found myself thinking, 'Yes, that was me, too!' Each essay leaves you smiling, nodding, or seeing your own life a little more clearly. I absolutely loved it and can't wait to carry it in my bookstore and share it with friends!"

—FRAN HAUSER, owner of Bedford Books and bestselling author of *The Myth of the Nice Girls*

"Zibby's memoir-in-essays is so real, so honest about marriage and having kids and work and community. Funny, brave, and sometimes heartbreaking—really, it's all the best adjectives."

—CAROLINE LEAVITT, author of *Days of Wonder*

"Like having coffee with an old friend—Zibby's essays are dishy, refreshingly honest, and true. Grab your cappuccino and catch up with Zibby in this fresh and funny new book."

—EILEEN HEISLER & DEANN HELINE, creators/ executive producers of *The Middle*

"A powerful collection of essays that captures, with precision and empathy, what it means to be a mother, a professional, and a creative person in today's world. This book left me feeling connected and inspired, a reminder to keep moving forward and embrace the risks that come with living fully. I can't wait to share it with readers who will be equally moved by its honesty and bravery."

—JEN BIRD, owner of Athena Books

"It's completely terrific. I absolutely love it."

—KATIE SISE, bestselling author of *You Must Be New Here*

"This collection of essays about parenting, writing, and, well, life is unflinchingly honest, eloquently written, and hard to put down. Save them for when you're in the mood to sit down with a friend and jump into her life for a little while."

—GAYLE WEISWASSER, co-owner and bookseller at Wonderland Books

"Zibby offers hope that it's never too late to revolutionize your life: build the career you've always dreamed of having, marry the person who brings out the best in you, and still raise resilient children. And she believes, as I do, that the comfort you seek can probably be found in your next book!"

—LAUREN CARDICK, owner of Matchmaker Bookshop

WRITTEN AND EDITED BY
ZIBBY OWENS

On Being Jewish Now:
Reflections from Authors and Advocates

Blank

Bookends: A Memoir of Love, Loss, and Literature

Princess Charming

Moms Don't Have Time to Have Kids: A Timeless Anthology

Moms Don't Have Time To: A Quarantine Anthology

BETWEEN CHAPTERS

How I Started Over, Took Some Chances, and Found the Plot

ZIBBY OWENS

ZIBBY PUBLISHING
NEW YORK

Between Chapters: How I Started Over, Took Some Chances, and Found the Plot

Published in the United States of America by Zibby Publishing, a division of Zibby Media LLC, 2026

Library of Congress Control Number: 2026939260
Paperback ISBN: 978-1-968506-90-2
eBook ISBN: 978-1-968506-12-4

Book design by Pauline Neuwirth
Cover photo © Zibby Owens

www.zibbymedia.com

Printed in the United States of America

10 9 8 7 6 5 4 3 2 1

To Mounjaro

Contents

Author's Note

I went through a period of extreme change from age thirty-nine to now, at almost fifty. *Fifty!* How?! Oh my gosh. As I shifted from being a stay-at-home mom of four kids to being recognized on the street for my work, from not being on social media to being an "influencer," from being married to divorced and then remarried, and from feeling relatively safe to realizing safety has been an illusion all along, I made sense of it through writing.

During that time, I fell in love, lost others I love, made mistakes, and got back up. I developed a stronger sense of voice, identity, and character. I tried new things, because if not now, when? I became a podcaster. An author. A bookstore owner. A publisher. An accidental activist. Even my name changed. Twice. I gained and lost weight, gained and lost friends. Like many of us, I also weathered natural disasters, societal turmoil, and the upside down of life as I knew it. And yet, as I went through it, I was building, creating something from what felt like nothing. Even a community.

What follows isn't me looking back wistfully on a disruptive time in my life. It's glimpses of me then, not knowing what would happen next. Some of the essays I shared publicly. Some I never have, until now. And many are new.

I didn't feel resilient as I wrote; I felt overwhelmed. So overwhelmed that I had to stop what I was doing, sit down, and write, which I've been doing since I was nine years old.

Sometimes doing so made me laugh. Sometimes it made me cry. But I always felt better afterward. It's only as I reread it all that I can sigh, pause, and say, *Wow. That was a lot.*

Why share it all now? It's one of those bookend moments in my life. The end of a chapter. My older daughter and son, twins, are headed off to college. My younger daughter is a newly minted teenager. My younger son is almost twelve. (Note: I don't name my children for privacy reasons. They can write their own stories later.) My "new" husband, Kyle, and I have been married for nine years. And I am turning half a century old. I wanted to pause here for a beat to reflect before immersing myself in the mayhem of what's to come.

I hope that by reading my experiences and perspectives, you'll feel empowered to get through whatever you're wrestling with today. Because we're all wrestling with something. I hope you'll laugh out loud, because if we can't find the humor in the madness of life, then forget it. I hope you'll feel more connected and understood, that you'll take some of the advice I give to my younger self, that you'll see that it's never too late to change. I also hope you'll consider turning to writing in tough times if you don't already. (You can contribute to the new *Between Chapters* platform at zibbyowens.com.)

So dip in, one essay at a time or all at once, between all the other things on your to-do list, between all the other books on your nightstand. You *must* get back to those.

But first, an interlude. I hope it helps.

Warmly,

Zibby

BETWEEN CHAPTERS

1

Forty Love

"Anything else, ladies?" the waiter asks.

"No, thanks! We're fine."

I'm at a moms' dinner at a loud, festive Mexican restaurant on the Upper East Side of New York City. I've just told this group of eight women that my husband of ten years and I are getting divorced.

"What?"

"Are you okay?"

Some of them are silent, covering their mouths in shock. Two of them lean forward and grab my hand, my arm, concerned.

"Zibby!"

It's clear they don't know what to say. I'm the most predictable mom of the bunch. I keep the activities of my four children organized by color-coded iCal calendars. I'm the first to sign up for after-school sessions and safety patrol. I wake up at 4:55 a.m. to register for parent-teacher conferences right at 5 a.m. when the link goes live.

Silverware stops clinking. Margaritas sit untouched. The moms stare at me. I'm leaving their ranks. I'm slipping away from what binds us together, being typical married moms. One of them starts crying.

"It's okay, ladies," I say. "Really. Thank you. It's okay. I'm okay."

"What can we do?" one says.

"Actually," I say slowly, "and this isn't *why* I'm getting divorced, but also . . . I'm in love. With someone else."

I can hear the collective intake of breath. These outgoing, vivacious, brilliant women who have been in the parenting trenches with me for years are stunned into silence. After years of playdates, class parties, school meetings, moms' nights out, harried morning coffees, and occasional lunches, we'd grown into a nice, supportive group. Now this.

Nancy, a hilarious Persian Jew with an infectious laugh and a fellow mother of four, is my closest friend in the group. We have gone on vacations together, shared many meals.

"What?" she says. "For real?"

"Are you joking?" another asks.

"No," a few say quietly, shaking their heads.

"You're serious?" Nancy says.

"Yes," I say. "I'm serious. This has all happened over a much longer time than it seems from this telling—in fact, years—but yes, now I'm in love. And I'm so happy. I've never been happier. I can't stop smiling."

Another long pause. I can see them processing what I've told them. I can hear their inner monologues. I can feel them dying to grab their phones to tell their own husbands, wanting to tell more people, reassessing their marriages. *Can you believe it?* I would've responded the same way; whenever I heard anything juicy, I would rush back to tell my ex, somehow feeling that would cement my own relationship, obscure any issues we faced. At least we weren't like *them.*

"Well, then, that's great," Nancy says, picking up her drink. *"Mazel tov!"*

The rest of the ladies just stare.

"So? Who is he?" she asks. I bite my lower lip.

"Brace yourselves, because this might sound kind of bad."

I am about to obliterate my image. I'm known for being responsible, serving on boards and committees, knowing which kids' classes are best, and getting all forms in on time. I'm straitlaced, type A, always busy. The one who does it all and always follows the rules.

I squint, bite my lip, inhale deeply, and say quickly, "He was my tennis pro." A brief pause.

Then the ladies start screaming, laughing, hitting each other, slapping the table, slumping over, cackling. It's too much.

"No!"

"Stop it!"

"Zibby!"

I'm laughing, too.

"I know, I know! It's like I'm in a movie. I'm a cliché."

Once they calm down, I say, "Look, I'm sorry I couldn't tell you anything before now. I know it's a lot. It was ridiculously hard to keep everything a secret. But we wanted to tell the kids about the separation first. Allow them to process everything."

"Are the kids okay?" another asks, concerned.

I quickly learn that people's reactions to my news reflect more about them and their own marriages than they do about mine. Over time, I see who feels really trapped. I hear whose husbands are cheating, which relationships are tenuous, who dreams of leaving. Marriages that have reconciled. The saying *You never know what goes on behind closed doors* has never felt more apt. Friends really start spilling when my divorce goes public.

"Wait," one of them says. "I need to know this. How *exactly* do you go about dating your tennis pro? I mean, how do you go from taking a lesson to the next step, if you know what I mean. How did you actually *do* that?"

So I tell them. I tell them the whole story. How it started with some innocent texts. The conversations over rallies during our lessons. The flirtation at the net with handshakes that lasted just a second too long. More texts. Meeting for a quick coffee before tennis. A few phone calls. His thoughtful birthday gift. The song he sent. A dinner. Some heart-to-hearts. A trip to the beach at night under the stars. Eventually, a passionate, unbelievable kiss in his parked car.

The moms are dying, drooling, mouths wide open. No one even checks their phone.

"Ladies, more drinks?" the waiter asks.

"We need a pitcher," Nancy quips.

The Upper East Side is actually a very small town when you've lived there for forty years. My news circulates quickly. Some friends, especially wives of my ex's friends, pull away.

One of my best guy friends won't email me back. A workout buddy gets *her* tennis pro to start talking smack about my tennis pro. A close girlfriend whose wedding I went to years earlier emails her husband snarky things about me, accidentally writing to me instead. The people who stand stalwartly by my side are both surprising and not.

No one really knows what went on in my marriage and I'll never talk or write about it. It's enough to know that it ended. That tennis came next. Yet people draw their own conclusions.

Years later, I marry Kyle on the tennis court at our rental house in the Hamptons under a chuppah, days after his conversion to Judaism was finalized. During cocktail hour, I will spin around in circles on the lawn in my strapless Vera Wang gown, layers of crinoline encircling me like the Sugar Plum Fairy, as I laugh. The kids will do cartwheels, play the guitar, dance, and sing. They will be more than okay.

Nancy and the moms from dinner will be at the wedding, holding hands and dancing the hora. The ones I care about the most will stay by my side. The guy friend who wouldn't email me back will apologize for how he behaved. Some wives of my ex's friends will ask me for coffee again. Meanwhile, Kyle and I will go on to have many new, interesting friends: athletes, musicians, producers, authors, screenwriters, architects, actors. Our creativity and happiness will attract new people.

Kyle will stop teaching tennis. He will start his own production company, making movies that resonate far and wide. He'll be a fantastic stepdad to my four kids, who have great relationships with him. I never think of him as a tennis pro; he's so much more than that. But we will play tennis for fun—and my forehand will get sensational. We'll have conversations during rallies. Flirt at the net. We'll eat family dinners at home that he cooks. He'll soon get his own color in my color-coded iCal calendar. Some of the moms in the group will fade into the background as our kids disperse to different schools.

But that night, as my inner circle laughs and glances at each other over bowls of guacamole and wonders what this will mean, I take it all in. I feel all the emotions. The guilt. The certainty. The love. The rescue. And I know that despite how torturous the past few months have been, I'll be okay.

2

I Had to Lie to Find True Love

I started lying when I fell in love.

My marriage was on the rocks when I began taking tennis lessons. But really *I* was the one on the rocks. My identity as a full-time stay-at-home mom of four didn't mesh with my perfectionistic, workaholic, creative personality.

I felt like an injured athlete stuck on the sidelines. Did anyone see *me* underneath the bibs and diapers, the paintbrushes and snack baggies? I could barely find time to read, let alone write, the activities that made me feel most *me*.

After having my twins, I'd tried for five years to have a third child, to no avail. After all paths had failed and I'd given away the baby furniture, I became quite unexpectedly pregnant. And then after I finished nursing my daughter, I found out I was pregnant again. It was like a joke. The younger two would be seventeen months apart. Four kids? How would I manage?

Anxiety veered sharply into depression, where it always

arrived if left unchecked. I was incredibly happy to be a mother, but I was also sinking. I cried often, hiding on the bathroom floor just to get a minute to myself. I was snapping at everyone. Overeating. Overtired. People I didn't know well asked, "Are you okay?" I wasn't.

The advice I kept getting—*keep going, come on!*—just wasn't possible. The crush of it was overpowering me. I felt like I was about to go under. I found myself fantasizing about getting into a car accident, canceling plans, developing physical ailments.

Enter tennis.

Soon my weekly lesson with Kyle, the dashing new pro in the Hamptons—a kind, warm, cute, and funny guy with an awe-inspiring tan—was the only thing getting me from nap time to bedtime. Something to look forward to. Where I could be me. For months, Kyle didn't even know how many kids I had. Over time I introduced him to them, bringing one in to share my lesson, another to wander around the court for fun. When he met my baby in the parking lot, he exclaimed, "There's another one?"

Our conversations weren't about the stresses in life. They were about the foods we enjoyed, courts we'd played on, songs we loved. The hour was filled with tactical, not emotional, advice: *Bend your knees, keep your eyes down, finish high, catch the racket.*

Across the net, I started to fall for Kyle, who, it turned out, was hilarious, smart, and endearingly innocent. He had just been recruited to the club after twelve years of coaching on the WTA tour, teaching lessons, and running major tournaments in the South. He was super close to his family, and he shared how he'd almost become a chef; his Italian family was full of restaurant owners, cooks, and professional bakers. Or possibly a hairstylist; he cut all his friends', his family's, and his own hair. But he decided to pursue tennis, which he started playing in high school only to strengthen his footwork as a star quarterback.

Kyle wasn't looking for anything to happen, either. So we connected with our guards down, soul to soul, enjoying each other's company, bantering nonstop, really understanding each other despite our completely different lives. He was dating someone new every week, going out late in Montauk, attending dinner parties of tennis clients, and working twelve hours a day without a break. He hadn't taken a vacation in more than a decade.

We got increasingly close all summer until we both realized: *Wait.* Neither of us wanted the lessons to end. Labor Day was coming, and I was heading back to the city with the kids. We started texting. Confessing. It was all quite innocent until the night I got the four kids down and left them with my sitter while I drove off to meet him for drinks. And then for dinner. The next week, the beach. The end of my marriage.

Getting separated and divorced was the hardest thing I'd ever gone through, a unique brand of grief. The pain of destroying my family unit, disappointing loved ones, disrupting everything stable, and knowing I would be sacrificing time with my children—which was how I measured my worth as a mother—to chase my own happiness made me physically ill. Was my happiness *worth* it? Would it last? Wasn't my job as a mom to suck it up and get through it? Who said I deserved to be any happier than I was?

Meanwhile, I was starting a real relationship with Kyle: kissing him in cars, giggling like a schoolgirl, and eventually sneaking off to hotels in the middle of the school day.

Aside from my best friend, Gen, our families, my ex, and the lawyers, no one knew. The school moms with whom I used to chitchat at kids' birthday parties, pickups and drop-offs, homeroom breakfasts, and baseball in the park were all off-limits. My whole social network in New York, where I'd grown up and still lived, was in the dark. I didn't want to tell anyone until everything was sorted and we could tell the kids about the separation.

One mom later told me she was convinced I was hiding a horrific medical condition given my significant weight loss, scattered mind, and inconsistent behavior. Used to being constantly open and authentic, I was suddenly, alarmingly, zipped up. I made excuses for why I couldn't attend this meeting or that coffee date.

And then there were the kids. The younger ones were too little to understand what was happening, but my twins picked up on everything. My daughter, then eight years old, was eerily perceptive.

"Who was the man on the phone?"

"Where are you going?"

"Why are you dressed up?"

"Why are you wearing *eyeliner*?"

"Where *were* you?"

My son grabbed my phone constantly, rifling through

photos, scrolling through my iPad for the latest app he wanted. The kids were like the K9 Task Force, sniffing out any scent of a device. I quickly became well-versed in hacks like hiding photos on my iPhone. I even went so far as to get *another phone*, but the kids found the box. I kept changing Kyle's name in my contacts to Unavailable or Wireless Caller or Unknown, even to Gen's name and my brother's, until my son picked up the phone one day before I could grab it and said a big "Hi, Uncle Teddy!" Then he paused, frowned, and asked, "Why did he hang up?"

Multiple therapists advised against telling the kids the truth *for their own good*; it was too soon. First, they had to get used to their parents separating. Divorcing. *Then* they could start to process someone new. Six months, maybe longer. Meanwhile I was going to parties with Kyle, starting to tell friends, publicly coming out, but the people I cared about most—the kids—didn't know.

Terrible mom didn't even begin to describe how ashamed I felt. I still couldn't eat because I was so upset leaving the kids on the days I didn't have custody. My life had collapsed, seemingly along with my morals. How much more would I have to sacrifice to change the course of my life? I knew I was ultimately doing the right thing for me and the kids, but it was clearly *not* the "right" thing.

Those crazy months in which my new life gestated before I told the kids about Kyle were rife with change. We moved homes in New York; I started using my maiden name again; friends who had aligned with my ex dropped me. I started spending a lot of time in LA, where my brother and his family lived and where I'd lived after college; the pain of being blocks away from my kids on their dad's custody days and not being allowed to see them was just too much. Sometimes it still is.

Kyle and I partially restarted our lives out west so I could be with my nieces and nephew when my own kids were off-limits and he could pursue a career in entertainment, which he had always wanted. I sobbed in my brother's kitchen on Thanksgiving after FaceTiming the kids, the turkey and sweet potatoes warm on the stove. It was a brutal, horrible time.

And yet I didn't regret it. I had to do it. Deep down I knew that I had to find joy and happiness or I wouldn't be able to be a parent at all, certainly not the way I wanted to.

The following Memorial Day weekend, my toes in the sand again and the therapist on board with the plan, I told the kids about Kyle, a secret I'd kept from them for nine months. I introduced them to him, and they also fell in love, some faster than others. I started eating again; Kyle even cooked for me—and soon for the kids, taking care of us. The lying could finally stop.

Kyle and I just celebrated our ninth wedding anniversary. What was once a dirty secret is now a source of pride and just a regular marriage. Over time, *how* it all went down became less important. But I knew I had found the strength to do something incredibly difficult, and I was willing to do it.

After everything, I am, indeed, happy. But I lied. I'm not proud of that, but I'm not sorry.

3

How Reading Helped Me Through My Divorce

When I got divorced at thirty-nine, with four little kids, I couldn't picture how my life was supposed to work. But every day kept coming anyway. As I pushed the stroller up and down Madison Avenue and raced across town to school pick-ups, my old, parallel existence was thrown into sharp relief, and the new world I'd just entered was still murky. Yet under the door that was now cracked open, I could see the tiniest bit of light shining through. I kept racing toward it.

The hardest part—there were and continue to be many hard parts—was having to share my kids, having to drop them off bimonthly. After protracted goodbyes, I would find myself standing on the street alone—and I would crumble. I could feel the sinking feeling in my gut, as if one of those boules thrown by old French men with cigarettes dangling from their lips had suddenly landed in my stomach. Plunk. In the rawness at the beginning, I would hide between parked cars to shield myself from the sure-footed march of pedestrians carrying on with their lives in ways that I found incomprehensible.

Joint custody. *Joint* is the worst word for it; I had never felt so *dis*jointed. Every joint in my body ached from the loss: My shoulders creaked, my knees and feet throbbed as I walked away every two weeks.

I did have Kyle, but our new relationship couldn't offset the feelings of loss every time the kids left. On my therapist's leather couch in a cramped office off Lexington Avenue, I would loudly shift in my seat to grab a tissue, horns blaring just beyond her window. The hole in my heart wasn't closing. Nothing was helping as I wandered past the kids' empty bedrooms on those quiet nights when they were gone. Should I keep their doors open or closed? I would stop occasionally to sit with the stuffed animals on my son's armchair and cry in the dark.

"You love reading. Read more books," my therapist said, sitting cross-legged on her armchair, still in her spinning clothes. "With a good book, you'll never be lonely."

While I'd always been an avid reader, as a newly divorced mom I threw myself into bibliotherapy. Reading was the only thing that could keep me from feeling the heart-shattering absence of my kids. Instead, I felt the delightful introduction to hundreds of characters dancing around in my mind, stories that entertained me, inspiring tales of others who had overcome injury, illness, addiction. I would plow through multiple books each weekend. When I married Kyle, my friends threw me a "book shower."

And then, in the middle of the ground reshuffling, I started a literary podcast so I could interview those authors. I wanted to hear more, directly from them. I had questions. While there were professional reasons for the podcast, perhaps the truest one was that it was a response to that sinking feeling I navigated every other weekend without the kids.

Years later, I'm in our bright, happy kitchen laughing with Kyle, his sister, Stefanie, father, Bernard, and stepmother, Miriam. We're cleaning up after dinner, wiping down the counters, clanking dishes in the dishwasher, and rinsing wineglasses with jazz playing and snow falling outside.

During dinner, I'd been texting with my older son under the table and had just FaceTimed with my older daughter. Technology was keeping us all closer on those weekends apart. That, and time, was helping to dull the ever-present ache.

Bernard picked up one of the books I was reading. I could see him trying to figure out where to safely put it down as we cleaned, food remnants on every surface.

"Everywhere I look, there's a book!" he said, chuckling. "Really, what's with all the books? Is this some kind of book fetish? Look at this!"

I laughed so hard I had to clutch my stomach. It's true—we were surrounded by books. I'd gotten so many advance reader copies in the mail that I'd recently bought a library cart for the overflow.

With a good book, you'll never be lonely.

It worked.

4

A Mother's Right to Sanity

There are days that I long for simpler times of parenting, when moms told their kids to be home for dinner and had no idea where they even went all afternoon.

Instead, I'm hunched over my phone, thumbs flying, trying to keep up with eight million kid-related emails, while also attempting to spend "quality time" with whichever kid I'm currently shuttling somewhere. How did we get here?!

I'm a typical mom on the verge of a nervous breakdown. Managing the schedules of four kids at three schools feels like a full-time job. Mind you, some of this is absolutely my own doing: Why did I sign them up for football, gymnastics, soccer, and an animal care class (!) if it's so stressful for me to get them all there on time? But how could I not? They'd be missing an enriching childhood experience! My kids would be deprived! Behind! Understimulated! Argh!

Never mind the fact that in the unstructured time at home,

they're almost never bored. The other day, my little ones spent over an hour pulling each other around the living room on a broom, laughing hysterically. The laundry "claw" is the hottest "toy" we have.

My inbox is a joke. Every class has a curriculum night, a parents' cocktail party, a moms' coffee, and parent-teacher conference. All classes have some sort of special snack, event, or donation that would be absolutely life-ending for my kids if I forgot it, like bringing a stuffed animal for assembly or donating the box of required rice for the school picnic. Rice! I just added an iCal event for the days when Eli the stuffed elephant will be coming home from school with us. Those 1950s moms didn't even have email!

Plus, it's not only their schools. Every single activity seems to have an orientation, a parent viewing class (with medals!), and required outfit changes. *This week, wear black shorts and a white T-shirt!* Why? Why!

Class trips, chaperoning field trips, picture day, dress-up day, dress-down day, PA meetings, class meetings, the food allergy affinity group meeting, the winter carnival kickoff. I have so many overlapping events on my calendar that I can't even see what's underneath it all. Plus, I struggle to keep up with all the apps and WhatsApp groups I must subscribe to so I can, say, watch my daughter's science class in action or monitor my son's homework assignments.

God forbid I add anything for myself in my calendar, like going to the dentist for that tooth that's been electrifying me every time I eat. And hmm, why would I be eating? The stress of the 24/7 parenting vortex hardly ever ends, except for that tiny window from 10 p.m., after my oldest goes to bed, until around 11 p.m., when my youngest starts coming into my room saying he needs more water.

I could use that time to bond with my husband or deal with the six thousand photos that need organizing, but instead I usually hit the pantry. My go-to right now is animal crackers.

Meanwhile, I've never felt so dependent on an evening glass of wine. The other day, my doctor had to put me on an antibiotic.

"But," the doctor said, "you can't drink for three days when you're on it."

I waited to take that antibiotic for almost two weeks until I could bear to part with my coveted evening drink.

I used to love working out, but with the kids' athletic practices and sports classes, my workouts are basically just the sprint to get everyone places on time. I know that even thirty minutes on an elliptical would make me feel better, but usually the second I hop on, I'm fielding calls from the school nurse, the doctors' offices confirming appointments, and after-school programs until I realize I haven't heard a single song on the headphones I rescued from my older daughter's trash heap of a desk drawer. Now it's time to pick up my son from preschool.

I am beat. I am throwing in the towel: you know, the one with my daughter's preprinted name tag label affixed to it. I don't even have time to shave my legs anymore. Mani-pedis? We're talking annually. Forget my eyebrows. Somehow, I still manage to look put-together, but inside I'm a mess.

There has only been one night in the last four years that no kids have woken me up, at least on my nights of the custody schedule. The other morning in bed, as I reached over to check an email about a kids' playdate while digesting another note from my ex, my new hubby reached over and tried to put his hand up my shirt. Are you kidding me? I'm like in mom ninja warrior mode here!

In fact, with the two little ones wandering in every night—no matter what failed methods I've tried to get them to stay in their beds—it's practically impossible to have sex. How do any relationships survive this parenting overdrive? I know I'm "lucky" in that Kyle and I get to spend time together every other weekend when my ex has the kids, but I swear, if we didn't, I don't know how we'd make it. And I'm madly in love with him.

Having kids today—perhaps worse with multiple kids, perhaps worse in New York City, but who knows?!—is a recipe for marital discord and psychological catastrophe. But what can be cut out? I'm not sure.

Maybe moms could tag team some of the events. "Hey, if you cover my curriculum night and write my kid a note, I'll take both our parent-teacher conferences next week." Maybe we could ask the schools to tone down the communications and events. Maybe I should start skipping it all. But then I'd never get to interact with anyone who doesn't watch *Paw Patrol.* Maybe I should kick up my heels and talk to my friends on the phone, 1950s style, while the kids zone out in front of the TV. I almost never get to talk to my friends anymore except the ones doing the same drop-offs and pickups, but thank God for those moms because without a little venting, I wouldn't be able to make it through each day.

The thing is, I had all these kids because I adore kids, especially mine, and I want to *be* with them, snuggle with them, laugh with them, play. I don't want to be so wrapped up in managing their lives that I can't sit on the floor in the afternoon and have a tea party. That's why I signed up for the stay-at-home-mom gig, not to use my MBA skills to organize class car pools.

I think there needs to be a movement to reclaim a mother's (or father's) right to sanity, even a mother's right to play with the kids without getting hopelessly behind on texts and emails. A mother's right not to constantly deal with school reminders, newsletters, and lice-check alerts. I don't want to be so busy all the time managing the kids that I can't just *be* with them.

Parenting shouldn't be this much of an office job, every day filled with forms and sign-ups, spreadsheets and logistics management. Moms need a break from it all so we can be good moms, the caregivers we long to be, not stressed executives at home, too.

Yesterday, I got a school email to bring in empty toilet paper rolls for a class project. No. No! I'm not doing it. I can't do it anymore. If that makes me a bad class mom, sign me up.

5

Finding My Voice

There's a home movie of my fourth birthday party that shows me bursting into tears and running away when my mother brought out my cake. I couldn't stand the attention. For many years, my dad had a framed picture of me on his nightstand. In it, I was peeking out a little from behind his leg, holding onto him for dear life.

As I got older, I found it hard to talk in groups. I mean, if I was *really* comfortable with everyone, I could be myself: outgoing, friendly, and chatty. But in new situations or big crowds, especially with *boys*? Forget it. I couldn't get any words out.

But that didn't mean I wasn't thinking. In fact, by not talking as much, I was able to look and learn, take things in, keep notes about everything in my head, sometimes even make myself chuckle.

It frustrated me that I had all these thoughts and ideas, but I couldn't find a way to share them with others. And then I discovered writing. I had always loved to read. I was the kid at summer camp who stayed inside and read a 300-page novel instead of playing dodgeball. I devoured books like candy. (Well, I devoured a lot of candy, too.)

When I got my first journal, I put my no. 2 pencil to the paper and words magically flowed out of me onto the page. Thoughts that had swarmed around in my head came pouring out in an organized, coherent way. I couldn't believe it. I could hear the melody behind the words and didn't want to turn it off.

In third grade, I wrote a short story about a set of twins who discovered a magic house and an essay in the style of author Rudyard Kipling. My step-grandfather, a miniature book publisher (yes, that's a thing) and rabbi, and my grandmother "Gagy" published my stories as a gift for my tenth birthday. I thought it was the coolest thing ever to be able to hand out my little books to friends and family. My name was on the spine. I was hooked. *This* was what I wanted to do with my life: be an author.

In middle school, my shyness hadn't really decreased—in fact, seventh and eighth grade were the worst as I lingered on the outside of groups, mute. I was excited to start over at a new school for high school, until I got the terrible news: Before classes started, I would have to go on a mandatory overnight trip to Frost Valley with the entire freshman class. Are you kidding me? I couldn't think of anything worse.

The trip was tough. I could barely speak for almost two days straight. In fact, during one of the last meals, I was sitting at a long table in the cafeteria when the teachers called for a moment of silence. Another girl sitting at the end of my table called out, "This shouldn't be hard for you, Zibby; you never talk." Everyone snickered. I wanted to disappear. Instead, I cried silently into my napkin.

Soon after I went to my new school, my parents got divorced. To cope, I ate a lot to make myself feel better. I ended up gaining twenty pounds, and, unsurprisingly, it didn't make me feel any better.

People were starting to treat me differently because of my weight. One afternoon, after a man on the street called me "big girl" as I walked by, I wrote a long diary entry about my body. My mom found it, read it, and told me that I should submit it to a magazine. She thought it would help a lot of other girls who felt the same way. So I did.

Shockingly, an editor at *Seventeen* magazine loved it and agreed to publish it. She even paid me. I didn't know you could get paid for writing articles—and it was a lot more than I got babysitting. I was asked to go down to the *Seventeen* office for a photo shoot, where the team plucked my eyebrows for the first time, plastered makeup on me, styled my hair, and posed me holding a scale in disgust. The piece came out when I was sixteen years old.

My essay was personal, a bit embarrassing, and totally honest. People loved it. My editor at *Seventeen* told me they'd never gotten more fan mail. Kids at school took me aside and thanked me, confessing that they felt the same way. They did?

The *Seventeen* experience changed my life. It made me realize that the time I'd spent being shy and watching rather than speaking was worth something. I could articulate myself on paper clearly because I'd spent so long *thinking* about everything. And I seemed to have a knack for writing really, really quickly.

I ended up writing wherever I went, starting at college. I edited a book while I was there, interned at a magazine, wrote for my business school newspaper, and then landed national bylines at *Redbook*, *Marie Claire*, *Shape*, and *Self*. While on bed rest, pregnant with twins, I even ghostwrote a fitness/fashion book that was published soon after they were born.

The best part of writing was knowing that I was helping people. I was helping them feel less alone. They could relate. They could connect. I wrote about everything from how sad I was that my local market had closed and I couldn't get my favorite corn muffins to showing up at a wedding wearing the same dress as all the bridesmaids.

As I've gotten older and more experienced, my shyness has slowly slipped away, almost without my noticing. I can walk into a room of strangers and have a normal conversation. I'm myself around almost everyone. People I meet now would never know that I used to be painfully shy, that I spent an entire summer program at age fourteen in France unable to speak to my peers except during required French lessons and instead spent the summer studying conversation patterns, marveling at the ease with which others spoke. I couldn't figure out how to just jump in. So I watched. Listened. Learned.

I continue to learn by staying quiet and listening while interviewing authors on my podcast. I've turned my shortcoming into a talent of sorts. Still, I'm grateful to writing for allowing me to find my speaking voice on the page. And I'm grateful to everyone who reads an article of mine and tells me afterward that it helped them in some way. Nothing makes me happier.

Remember that mean girl from Frost Valley? She left my school, while I stayed, made tons of great friends, cocaptained three sports teams, became photo editor of the yearbook, wrote for a national magazine, and found my voice. Moment of silence girl, eat your heart out.

(Note: After I gave a version of this speech at my kids' school, another mom came up to me and suggested we get coffee. It was bestselling middle-grade author Sarah Mlynowski. At coffee, I told her about the book I was trying to sell, a collection of parenting essays called *Moms Don't Have Time to Read Books.* She didn't think that was the right project. "Let me think about it. I'm good at helping people with their careers," she said. A few days later, I was leaving the school and she was coming in. "A podcast!" she said. "You should start a podcast!" And so, I did.)

6

Let's Lose Weight Later

When I was in my twenties, I was a Weight Watchers Leader. As a "lifetime" member who had successfully achieved her goal weight and then stayed there for six weeks, I was eligible to become a meeting-room receptionist and then, after months of training, a meeting leader. Armed with the tools I'd acquired at a mandatory weekend retreat in New Jersey, I was running easel-style meetings in fluorescent-lit basements, in high-rise corporate offices, and in people's homes. I was the one teaching members tricks and strategies for losing weight and keeping it off. Ironic, after years of yo-yo dieting.

My goal was to help women like me who had struggled with weight their whole lives. I felt like I'd finally found the holy grail of weight loss—the Points system!—and wanted to share the Kool-Aid. Although I'd "only" lost twenty-five pounds, I felt like the program had changed my life forever. Suddenly my most public failure, not being able to control how much I ate, was gone.

Most meeting leaders were older than me and had lost significantly more weight. For many, leading meetings had become their full-time job. I showed up in a new size two Theory pantsuit in my twenties and didn't exactly fit in. When I look back at how worried I used to get about eight-tenths of a pound, I could punch myself in the face.

Tons of moms used to come to our Upper West Side location. There was a constant parade of yoga-pant-wearing stroller-pushers, lamenting how hard it all was.

"There's so much tempting food at kids' birthday parties!"

"I snack on their meals and never eat my own!"

"I don't have time to cook or plan healthy meals!"

"Come on, you can do it!" I urged them, not truly understanding. "Plan ahead! Make weekly menus. Log what you eat. Don't eat at birthday parties—save it for later. Who needs cake at four p.m., anyway?"

I'd give my little spiel about how easy weight loss could be ("I mean, look at me!") and they'd just stare back at me with a mix of disgust and exhaustion. And never come back.

At that time—newly married, out of business school, before trying to have children—what I ate and when was firmly in my control. My environment was calm, quiet, and predictable, so I could focus on losing the pounds that had crept up on me, working out daily, cooking nightly.

Fast-forward to now, four kids later. I don't think those suits would even fit over my left leg. I weigh more today than I did in my "before" pictures when I joined Weight Watchers.

I want to apologize to those Upper West Side moms for being so completely naive. I get it now. It feels impossible. I'm so sorry!

What I didn't understand then was that eating cake at kids' birthday parties would sometimes be the highlight of my day. A victory was managing not to also eat my son's cake and that of the kid next to him when no one was watching.

Meal planning? Yeah, right. It's all I can do to not feed the kids the same thing every evening. I never want to see a taco again. And dinner happens every night! I can't cross it off the list! Plan my own meals, too? You've got to be kidding.

I tried to do Weight Watchers online recently, but every time I went to track my food on the app, I'd get distracted and end up dealing with one of my 86,000 kid-related emails. I couldn't even remember what I'd had for breakfast. Did I have breakfast?

My environment now is the opposite of what it was. It's noisy with four kids, babysitters, family, and friends going in and out all day. It's fast-paced and hectic. A crisis always needs handling. Someone's usually yelling. Something needs finding. I'm constantly sleep-deprived, a huge cause of overeating.

But, like many moms, I don't see a clear path to changing any of it other than time simply passing. Now even my larger-size clothes are getting tight. I stand in the kitchen after bedtime, pantry cabinet door open, mindlessly eating—food into mouth, repeat—to decompress from the day. To have something only for me, the moment, the time, the treat.

I want to lose weight, but I can't bear to give that time up. And I'm not replacing it with something unrealistic that experts recommend, like a soothing bath. You think I want to deal with another bath and confront my naked body after the day I've had?

No. I want a hit of sugar. Pure white. Now. Bring it.

As moms, we care for everyone else all day. And all night. There's no "time off," really. There's hardly any space to relax and get our needs met, no lying on the couch for hours watching *Gossip Girl* while nibbling on four cups of carefully measured microwave popcorn.

But what I've realized is that unless I find a way to do a tiny bit more for myself, I can't show up the way I want to for my kids. I'll waste my most precious commodity—my headspace—worrying about my weight when I need to be focused on sending my daughter to her activity on the correct day or figuring out which kid still needs a flu shot.

If I could go back to the Weight Watchers meetings, I'd tell those moms: It's okay. It won't always be this hard. You'll eventually have time again when you're in control, when you can work out and eat right. For now, enjoy the time with your kids when you can. Celebrate that your body produced your children. Buy clothes a few sizes bigger than what you want and don't freak out about it. Eat cake at birthday parties. We all need a little something. We deserve it.

(Note: If only I'd known then that Mounjaro was on the horizon!)

7

Holiday Gifts

I think it needs to come out right away," my doctor says, looking at the ultrasound screen.

The plastic wand slides over my stomach like a beginner at an ice rink, jerking this way and that, stopping occasionally. The jelly oozes over my bare skin, reminding me of all the ultrasounds I've had, facilitating the exits of my children.

This one is different.

My doctors have been watching my small uterine fibroid for years as it has grown, bit by bit, never large enough to warrant much attention. No symptoms. Just a benign tumor in my uterus, a collection of tissues and muscle cells. And yet, I feel constantly bloated. I look pregnant.

It's right after drop-off in early December, smack-dab in the middle of holiday chaos: Hanukkah shopping, school concerts, holiday-card addressing, and parties. I'm under the bright, unforgiving lights in a small exam room, listening to my breath go in and out. Waiting. The wand.

"Yeah, it has to come out," the specialist says. "The rapid growth is suggestive of it no longer being benign. Let me see when the next opening is on my schedule."

No longer benign. So, malignant? *Cancerous?* Is that what she was saying?

The doctor takes the condom off the wand, throws it in the garbage, and walks toward the door, the clicking sound of her high heels out of place in this disinfected sanctuary.

"Hopefully we can do it laparoscopically, but we won't know until we get in there."

Wait, what?

My fibroid is now as big as a grapefruit. It redecorates my insides, moving organs into new places, changing the design. And it might be cancerous.

I get dressed hastily. I don't have time for surgery. I don't even have time to *make an appointment* for surgery. Although if the fibroid is cancerous, who even cares about all the little things? If the fibroid is cancerous, then that's it. My "to-do list" would be permanently undone, a joke. And what about my kids? Something bad happening to me that leaves them without a mother is my deepest, darkest fear. The very thought of it inspires intense panic attacks that jolt me upright in the middle of the night, gasping for air, sweating. Could that really be happening now?

I walk down the corridor into the doctor's small, warm, carpeted office, overflowing with books, and sit down at her wooden desk.

"We'll do the hysterectomy next Wednesday," she says, her eyes on her screen. "I don't think we'll have to take the ovaries."

Wait. She isn't talking about taking out the fibroid. She's talking about taking out my entire uterus.

I start peppering her with questions: what that means, whether I'll go into menopause, what recovery looks like, how the whole process works. My December vacation plans go up in smoke. The family trip to Jamaica. The week-long escape when the kids go to their dad's. I picture myself ripping up old-school plane tickets, the shreds fluttering slowly down to the ground. I see the holiday assembly. My daughter's school play. The gymnastics awards. My empty seat. Everything I'll have to miss.

It's easier to think about the short-term logistics than what it would mean to have cancer. To *die* from cancer. Like my dear preschool mom friend, dying of ovarian cancer and leaving behind her five children. Am I going to be next? I pick up the phone to text Kyle. My finger pauses above the screen. What can I say?

Days later, I'm being wheeled unconscious on a stretcher through Mount Sinai Hospital, still under anesthesia. I find out later, I'm pushed into an elevator with strangers who are checking their phones, texting. I've just had a four-and-a-half-hour surgery. The fibroid was bigger than they thought. My organs were stuck together from my previous C-sections and had to be filleted apart, the specialist expertly separating them like a sushi chef. I imagine her doing this still in her high heels.

Kyle, my mom, and my best friend, Gen, are two floors above me. Waiting. Kyle paces. My mother talks and talks, telling so many stories about me that Kyle finally says, "Hey, it's not her funeral!"

Gen has taken the train in from Philly, missing work, to be there for just a couple of hours until she races back to her kids' school pickup and a hockey tournament. I'll see her for two minutes before she has to go. No one expected the operation to take so long. To hurt so much.

I wake up and see her smiling face.

"You did it, Zwibble! I love you. Gotta run."

Then Kyle, leaning over me.

"My honey, my honey," he says, looking into my eyes. "Are you okay?" He looks so scared.

My mother starts ordering everyone around behind us, wanting me to be moved upstairs.

I can barely talk.

"Was it cancer?" I whisper.

"Not cancer," my husband says softly, smiling. I fall back asleep.

I'm at home in bed. My kids snuggle under the covers with me in the early morning, the TV on. It hurts to move. The pain comes in waves, taking my breath away, making me grimace, grabbing anything nearby to squeeze. The little ones don't really understand, of course. I load up on painkillers. They don't like to see Mama in pain. My twins barely slow down, popping in and out, asking me to sign school forms from bed. I'm typically a whirling dervish in the mornings: a short-order cook, a fashion consultant, a luggage handler, a logistics coordinator. Now I'm trying, and failing, to do it all from bed.

"Don't forget your leotard!" I yell to my daughter as she tromps down the stairs.

"Show me your homework! Wait!" I scream at my son who is attempting to leave without my signing his planner as parents are instructed to do.

I feel ancient, way past my fortyish years, robbed of that central piece of motherhood machinery. Barren. The absence of my uterus aches in ways that far exceed the surgery. Am I even still a woman? I reflect on my gender, my body, rewriting the script. Soon, I'll go into early menopause, hot flashing at dinner tables, holding my arms out like I'm a toy soldier, waiting for the moments to pass. My hair will start falling out. I'll be moodier, more tired. Years later, my shoulder will freeze. I'll be at a college visit with my older son and while pulling out a sleeper sofa, I'll mention, "So funny. I can't raise my arm beyond my shoulder."

"What do you mean?" he'll ask.

"I don't know. Look." And I'll hold out my arm.

"Just lift it more!"

"I can't. That's why I'm mentioning it."

He'll shake his head. "You should see a doctor, Mom."

"I think it's called frozen shoulder. From menopause."

"Too much information."

But now it's Christmas Eve. The kids have left for a week with their dad. I stand alone in the playroom, the recently opened Hanukkah gifts balancing precariously in discarded piles. Will the kids even remember what they got when they return? Only their begrudgingly written thank-you notes might jog their memories. The house is so quiet. Still. The chaos and screaming and laughter are suddenly on mute.

I want to cry. I can't bring myself to glance into their rooms.

Suddenly I get the idea to donate many of the kids' gifts to children who are stuck in the hospital that Christmas. I pull down the wrapping paper rolls from the closet shelf, grab a little-kid pair of scissors, Scotch tape, and slowly get on my hands and knees, grimacing. I wrap the unopened gifts, folding, cutting, ripping, slicing. I put on music. Sound fills the room again. I handwrite a holiday card for the patients, photocopy it, tape one to each present.

Hours later, when I've finished the whole task, Kyle and his father, Bernard, whisk them off to make the daily drop-off deadline at the hospital.

I creep back downstairs and slowly crawl into bed. I've aggravated the wound. It hurts. I'm alone in the house again under the cool sheets. *Silent night.* And yet I feel so full, knowing I've given back even when something was taken away from me.

I shut my eyes. *All is bright.*

This holiday season, *naughty or nice* takes on a different meaning. This time, my body is the one being naughty, hiding things from me the way I used to hide Hershey's Kisses from the local deli under my bed. My body is breaking the rules, rebelling, forcing me to jettison fundamental parts of myself. *Nice* is all I have left. To be nice. To think of others. To brighten their holiday when mine is so dark. To connect.

The hospital coordinator sends me a picture the next day, on Christmas. A group of kids, brought together by their own body betrayals, are holding our presents, smiling ear to ear, a hospital worker in a Santa costume next to them.

"Thank you!" they say.

Naughty or nice.

I can't help my body's naughtiness, but I can choose to be nice.

8

The Birds and the Bees

We sat in the back row. It was embarrassing enough to be attending the fourth grade "Growth and Development" evening at my son's school with Kyle. I certainly didn't need to be front and center.

"Okay, everyone," the ponytailed twenty-something health teacher said from the front of the library. Did she even have kids?

"We're going to be covering a lot of information that we'll be teaching your kids this spring. For starters, we're going to emphasize calling all the body parts by their real names, not the cutesy nicknames you might have been using. Who would like to share some nicknames you use now?"

Kyle nudged me with his knee, as if that would convince me to raise my hand in front of sixty other parents and yell out, "Weenie!"

Thankfully, no one said a word. The teacher continued and introduced the team who would be tackling this tough subject with our kids. The third-grade assistant teacher jumped up and started telling us all about his sexual education in Catholic school and how he would handle things differently with our kids.

"They showed us a video, gave us a banana and a condom, and said 'good luck,'" he recounted, stone-faced. And then sat down again.

Um, okay.

"Don't worry!" the cheerful health teacher said. "We don't teach that type of thing until eighth grade and we don't use bananas."

Kyle leaned over to me.

"What do you think they use instead?" he whispered.

"The ninth graders," I said.

He burst out laughing. We tried to ignore the disapproving glances all around us.

After presenting an amusing little video in which awkward parents tried to explain sex to their kids, the health teacher said she would be emailing us a video for us to watch with our children.

"We'll be showing the students this movie about puberty in class right after spring break," she said. "But it might be helpful to watch it together first and go over any questions your kids might have. We'll be emailing you all a lot of resources."

I made a mental note to show my twins the movie as soon as I got the email. I knew they would be heading to their dad's for the first week of vacation and I wanted to watch it with them before they went away. I'd already explained the "facts of life" to both kids individually.

My daughter had simply responded, "I did *not* need to know that."

So that's how, at 8 p.m., I ended up in my blue fluffy robe and jammies, squeezed in between my son and daughter on my son's bed, with my laptop precariously balanced, all our shoulders touching, watching the "movie."

Every so often, I would freeze the video to make sure they understood.

"Okay, so which of you has testosterone and which of you has estrogen?"

"Do you see how the egg is released and goes down the tube into the uterus?"

Occasionally, they'd ask me a question. Like, when would puberty start? How would they know? Layups. I mean, how good a mom was I being? Watching the movie ahead of the class, bonding with the kids, being an open, reassuring resource for them. I was feeling pretty good about myself.

After we watched the movie, I clicked back to the school email to see if there was anything else I'd missed. Oh wait, the FAQs. I opened the next document and scrolled down the list of forty-four questions. Sure, I could totally explain these.

The kids got up and started wandering around the room as I read out the questions. My son started punching his new punching bag while my daughter practiced her gymnastics splits on the floor. I read the questions out loud and then answered them. Yes, I noticed the questions in the document were all formatted in a bold and blue font, but it didn't occur to me that they were all hyperlinked to paragraphs of preapproved answers. I answered on the fly, figuring that's what I was supposed to do.

We quickly got into some tricky territory.

"FAQ: What's an erection?"

Oh God. I started explaining.

"You know, you need to have an erection to have sex."

The kids just looked at me.

"I mean, the penis doesn't just go into the vagina the way it is now," I said. Points for using the real body part names!

"It has to be . . . uh . . . hard."

"Oh, you mean stiff?" my son said.

"No, it's called being hard."

"Why? Can't we say 'stiff'?"

"No."

"Why not?"

"I don't know! That's just not what it's called."

"But what if it's not hard?"

"Well, sometimes you can do things to get it that way."

I was beginning to feel very uncomfortable. I looked back at my list of FAQs. Next up was: "What is oral sex?" I guess I was supposed to be tackling all this, too. Seriously?

"Like what?" my son asked. Oh boy.

"Well," I said, watching my daughter doing backbends. "You can, well, you can touch it to make it hard. Or the woman can help."

"Help?!" my son exclaimed, incredulous. "What do you mean? How can she help?"

Holy crap. Now what? I bit my lip and could feel my face start flushing. Maybe I should've left this for their dad after all. I took a deep breath.

"The girl can touch it, too. It's called giving a hand job."

"Ewwwww!" they both shouted. My daughter couldn't stop laughing.

"How exactly though? Just, like, holding it?" my son asked.

Christ. How much detail did I have to go into? Next thing you know, I'm sitting there, imitating giving a hand job in the air in front of my twins. They couldn't stop laughing. This felt very, very wrong.

But I still had to tackle the next question. *Just get it over with,* I told myself.

"You can also do it another way and that's called oral sex," I said. "Which is when the woman puts the penis in her mouth. That's called a blow job."

Silence.

The kids froze in their tracks on opposite sides of the room. Then, in complete synchronicity, they burst out laughing again. They were both literally doubled over when my son suddenly looked up and said, "Wait! Did *you* do that? Did you do that to Dad?"

Oh God, now what?! I sat there trying to figure out how to dig myself out of this monster hole.

"You did!" my son screamed. "I bet you did!"

He then jumped up and ran over to the phone.

"I'm calling Dad to find out!"

"Noooooo!" I yelled. "Put the phone down! Stop!"

I could only imagine my ex's reaction to getting this call.

Then my son froze, the wheels turning in his brain.

"Wait a minute, now you're married to Kyle. So now do you do that to Kyle?"

Oh. My. God.

"Now I know what you're doing in your room!"

My daughter and I were laughing so hard at this point that tears were streaming down our faces. I couldn't even sit up.

"Stop it!" I begged my son again. "I didn't say I did or I didn't! I was explaining what it means and what people do when they love each other. And it's private! You don't talk about it to anyone!"

"I'm going to find out," my son said.

"Okay, enough FAQs for tonight," I said, slamming my laptop closed and jumping off the bed. "But you know, you have to get the woman's permission to do anything. You can never force someone to have sex—or even touch someone—who doesn't want you to. That's called rape. Have you heard that word? And you'll go to jail forever. Do you hear me? Jail. Forever!"

I could kind of hear Kyle walking toward us from down the hall and then turning around and hightailing it out of there.

Later, with some warning about what happened, Kyle went up to say goodnight to my son, where he was promptly asked, "So, does Mom suck your penis?"

Kyle just shook his head when he came back down again.

"Aren't the kids really young to be learning about all this?" he asked. "They don't really seem to be ready."

"I know, but it was in the FAQs!" I replied. "I just went down the list of questions from the school! It wasn't my idea! I'm supposed to be teaching them about all of this before they learn the rest in class. I mean, at least I decided to stop at anal."

"I don't know, honey," he said. "I didn't hear about this stuff until I was much older."

"Me too, actually," I realized. I hadn't even heard the term "blow job" until the seventh-grade rumor mill.

I opened up the FAQs again while sitting at my desk in our library. "Look!" I showed Kyle.

He got up from the armchair where he'd been watching tennis on TV and leaned over my shoulder to look at my laptop.

"Scroll down," he said. "Or click on the links."

The links? I clicked.

The document jumped down to the school-approved answer, which was: *Tell your child that there are lots of ways to show love, but this is something we'll get into more in 7th or 8th grade.*

Oh no.

I ruined them.

I started laughing so hard that it hurt.

"Honey," Kyle said, shaking his head, as I laughed uncontrollably.

"I totally messed up!" I cried. "Oh my God."

The next morning, when the kids and I were in the back seat of a taxi driving to school, I said, "Oh! You know the end of our conversation last night? Well, apparently, I wasn't supposed to go into all those details until seventh or eighth grade."

"Which part?" my son asked, looking out of the window. "The hand job or the blow job?"

The cab driver glanced back at me, horrified, in the rearview mirror.

The next day, the kids switched over to stay at their dad's

house. I emailed my ex before they arrived forwarding all the "resources" the school had sent me with a note saying, "You might want to review some of this before the weekend. The kids watched the video. You could be in for some priceless questions."

My ex emailed me back: *Too late.*

9

Family Trips

I saw an old video of myself the other day. I was packing for an upcoming trip and my twins, who were about two years old then, were circling around me. I don't remember where we were going, but what has stuck with me is how, on camera, I seem like a contestant on a reality TV competition. My hair is flying and my brow is furrowed as I appear in and out of the frame, grabbing clothes, zipping and unzipping duffel bags as I shove things in. Head down. The twins, meanwhile, keep trying to get my attention.

"Mama, look!"

"Mommy, come here!"

I was in a full-bodied packing haze, completely consumed by the stress of packing for our whole family: the wipes, the diapers, the shoes, and the books. Did I remember his favorite socks? Her bathing suit?

Watching my younger self, at first, I'm horrified. In my zeal to make the kids happy at every stage of the upcoming trip, to anticipate all their needs while *away from home,* I was ignoring them *at home.* All I had to do was meet their gaze, give them a quick squeeze, and then go back to what I was doing. But I couldn't even manage that. I'd missed the plot.

Despite all the prep before our trips when they were little, I still made mistakes. I forgot my daughter's beloved "bearies" and begged family friends to reroute their own trip to swing by our home and pick them up. I only packed goggles for one kid—a true crime with twins—and once I forgot diapers for my younger daughter, so I ended up taking the kids to their first Walmart. There, my older daughter stood in the doll aisle with her mouth wide open and screamed, "I love this place!"

Now the kids are old enough to pack themselves. After our trips, I don't reminisce about what I packed or lament what I forgot to pack. I remember the times we laughed, the hugs, the adventures, the bedtimes, the moments. I know this now. And yet, back then, didn't the stuff still need to get packed?

I rue the dreaded advice to just be *in the moment* while simultaneously doing all the invisible labor required for the moment to go off without a hitch. Guess what: Every moment *isn't* worth remembering. And it's *impossible* to appreciate every moment, unrealistic to be *expected* to appreciate every moment. That's the part of life that everyone wrestles with: navigating the challenges and clinging to the joys knowing it will all end. Right?

Yes, I may have been too stressed packing that day. I'm sure I'd built in extra time and could've taken a few minutes to play with the kids. I should have stopped to look them in the eye and explain what I was doing and why I needed to finish. It was the least I could do. I wish I'd learned then how to manage my tendency to hyperfocus, my inability to move on until I complete a task on my list. But that's part of who I am and the reason I succeed in other areas.

I shake my head watching that old video. I was doing the best I could. I want to give my younger self a hug and tell her it would've been okay to forget something. I want to tell her that I see how much was on her plate, how the mental load of remembering everything for everyone in the family weighed on her, that she'll burn out if she keeps up at this pace.

I want to advise her to rate the importance of each task and its deadline before she starts it because all tasks aren't created equal. I'd tell her to adjust some of the self-imposed deadlines. And I'd tell her that sometimes, being *in the moment* means reveling in the imperfection of it all, finding the humor of the situation, and just getting through the day.

I'd whisper: *It gets easier. And you won't necessarily miss these moments.*

I long to show her iPhone videos from our recent trips. She wouldn't have believed it. She would've laughed watching us all clutch our seats on a rickety bus, lost in the Irish countryside. She would've laughed seeing us eat chicken fingers on the dirty floor of a dilapidated Catskills resort because my son wanted to go "upstate" to meet a girl. She would've laughed peering into a sketchy Pokémon-themed apartment in the middle of Tokyo that my kids had booked online. She would've laughed seeing us decked out in Taylor Swift apparel after we lost our car at the concert in London. She would've laughed at us covered in bug bites at a resort in the Cayman Islands, playing board games at the dinner table.

The kids all groan when I plan a trip knowing it will probably get messed up since I now plan things a bit last-minute—and change plans all the time. But they know that with that spontaneity, our trips have gone from stressful to hilarious. We vote on where to go, often in a Google poll my younger son creates. He planned our entire itinerary in Japan at age eight and I let him. Why? Because it doesn't matter what we do or where we go as long as we're all together.

That's what I want to tell the younger me from the video: that in sixteen years, you'll be in the airport with the kids, and *they'll* be leading the way. And you'll be smiling and laughing, too, even though you forgot to pack socks. Thankfully, there's always a Walmart nearby.

10

At a Bat Mitzvah the Night of the Pittsburgh Shooting

I went to a bat mitzvah a few hours after a dozen fellow Jews in Pittsburgh were brutally murdered during a bris, the Jewish ceremony of circumcision for baby boys. I remember the brises of my two sons like they were yesterday: how proud I felt, how terrified I was of hurting my newborn, how warm it felt to have my family gathered around us like a cocoon, and how comforting the Hebrew prayers sounded.

With every Jewish tradition, I always feel the reverberations of history—the echoes of all the boys' cries that have come before my own sons'. The idea that one hateful man could enter another family's sacred moment—in a synagogue, no less, a place so sacred I won't even enter without wearing a skirt—and slaughter the participants in cold blood is impossible for me to comprehend. And yet, it happened.

As Kyle and I sat in our study watching the news footage of

the worst attack on Jews in American history at that time, away from the prying eyes of my four innocent children, we talked about the horror of it all.

"Maybe no bat mitzvah tonight?" Kyle said. "Is it even safe to go?"

"We *have* to go," I responded. Not only did I want to be there to support my dear friend's first-born daughter, but I *needed* to be there. We must stand up to evil. We can't let fear win. We owe it to ourselves and other Jews to be brave. That's how we've gotten through thousands of years as a tribe. Right?

In the cab ride to the bat mitzvah that evening with my two older kids, then eleven years old, I decided I had to tell them what happened. I wanted to shield them from the news as long as possible. I wanted to shield them forever. From everything. But I thought it would probably come up in the service that evening.

While rain pelted the roof of the cab, the dark sky enveloping us, my son responded by taking a deep breath. He shook his head and asked, "Is anything like that going to happen here in New York?"

I responded honestly: "I hope not, love."

During the ceremony, at a beautifully decorated event space, seated on Lucite chairs, watching my friend's radiant, brilliant daughter delight in her big moment, her confidence, poise, and happiness emanating from the bimah, I found myself crying. I got goose bumps on my arms, imagining all the other b'nai mitzvah going on that night: the boys and girls around the world reciting the age-old Torah portions, the Hebrew letters floating above them like a cartoon, with loss coursing throughout.

As I stood to recite the Mourner's Kaddish, I tried to stop the tears long enough to chant. *Yitgadal, v'yitkadash, sh'mei raba.*

My daughter looked up and took my hand in hers, even stroking my arm a bit. She had, uncharacteristically, placed her preteen head on my shoulder for most of the service, sensing my distress.

Y'hei sh'mei raba m'varach l'alam ul'almei almaya.

What a time to be able to mourn with others in the community. I prayed silently for so much: for the families of those who had lost their lives, for the Pittsburgh community, for my Jewish community around the world, for our country. I sang all the prayers and recited the familiar blessings, the lullabies of my culture. At the end, I wiped away my tears with a tissue procured from a fellow mom behind me, hugged my kids and Kyle close, and headed to the celebration.

Before dinner began, the DJ asked all the kids to come onto the dance floor. I started dancing with them in a circle. Kyle yelled over the music: "You know we're the only grown-ups out here, right? I think this is just for kids!"

I didn't care. I danced next to my daughter in the crowd. Once the hora began, I was in the inner circle, hand in hand with friends and family, surrounded by circles of strangers as we raised our arms and toasted the bat mitzvah girl.

Hava, nagila, hava!

I took part in all of it, smiling, laughing, and celebrating the beautiful, brave, bat mitzvah girl as she cemented herself firmly in the Jewish tradition. The timing of this event will shape her, as so much else has in her young life. I was privileged to be a part of it, to show my kids that nothing will get in the way of celebrating our Jewish traditions.

Our community is stronger than that and always has been. One man's horrific decision will not tear us apart. I am so grateful that I had the ability that night to toast all that was right in the world: Love. Compassion. Family. Friends. The indomitable human spirit. Rituals. Tradition.

Community.

And, yet again, to never forget.

11

Journey Women

I met up with an old friend today to go to our rabbi's funeral. Maggie and I popped into a nearby coffee shop and slid into a booth in our matching black dresses—hers with a blazer, mine with a sweater and pearls. We hadn't seen each other in over a year. She'd had a baby: her third child. I'd gotten remarried. My older kids had started middle school. My little ones were almost too heavy to lift.

But the eternity since our last catch-up didn't matter—we resumed our conversation as if we'd just spoken the day before. That's how it always is with her. No matter how much time passes between our heart-to-hearts, it's like we never stopped chatting. We've known each other forever. She's like family.

As we went over the details of the funeral—the location of the shiva, the illness that had plagued our beloved rabbi David Posner, the dignified, warm, caring guardian of so many of our life events—we settled into an easy rhythm. Touching each other's arms to express surprise; commenting on what looked better about each other since our last coffee.

Maggie is one of the few people to whom I confess my innermost secrets. Years ago, at another neighborhood coffee shop, I'd walked in shaking, stunned from a particularly upsetting fight with a loved one that had rocked me to my core.

She'd said, "Okay, I can take it. What happened?"

Later, at another catch-up, she was the one I told that my ex and I were getting separated. She's the only one I grab when I pass her on the street and say things like: "I haven't showered in two days!" She doesn't judge, but says, "Try three."

As we talked today, joined together for the somber occasion, Maggie referred to me as one of her "journey women," someone who has stood by her for the long haul. She has been like that for me, too.

As I've gotten older, I've had to limit my time hanging out with girlfriends. Instead, I'm often sitting on my carpet, surrounded by sippy cups, watching *Young Sheldon* or maybe football with my husband, while I work on my computer. I've noticed that some of my friendships can withstand the infrequent watering—they're the evergreens in my friendship garden. The orchids—the friends that need more regular maintenance to stay alive—have started withering at the stems. And those that need excessive care, I've had to jettison.

I keep many wonderful friendships alive by throwing occasional parties or gatherings just to give these special girls a hug, a dose of sunshine, or to say how much I care, even though I haven't—and they haven't—had enough time to properly catch up. Spending time with girlfriends has become as big a treat to me as getting a massage: something I look forward to, that always makes me feel better for days afterward, and that I don't indulge in very often.

So many other things pile up on my desk, in my inbox, and on my plate, that the things I do *just for me* get pushed aside.

I glanced at my watch. Our coffee date was almost over; the funeral was starting soon.

We'd barely scratched the surface, comparing kids' summer programs, our latest injuries, our family issues, and more.

"It's time to go," I said.

"No! Already?"

"I know!"

She looked at her watch.

"Five more minutes," she said. "We can sit in the back."

Eventually, we walked down the street, bundled up against the cold but with our conversation to keep us warm. We walked into the synagogue, one of the largest in the world, and sat side by side in the cavernous space as we heard eulogies that made us cry, grip our chests, hug each other.

"I'm so glad we came to this together," she whispered.

"I was just thinking that," I whispered back.

We stood up for the Kaddish and watched the rabbi's children, who are our friends and have become parents themselves, wipe their eyes and greet other congregants. Rabbi Posner was carried out in a plain wood box.

We followed the procession outside. I had to rush off in one direction, Maggie in another. As we left the sea of mourners on the sidewalk, the distance between us grew. But that was only in the physical sense. In my heart she is always by my side. My journey woman.

12

Don't Crush My Butterflies

I was the only grown-up angling to get more fire on my marshmallow. Little kids shoved me out of the way as we jousted with our extra-long bamboo sticks for the perfect roasting position. It was my first vacation without the kids since I'd *had* kids, and there I was around a firepit in Puerto Rico, packed in with everyone else's.

Kyle and I were still at the butterfly stage of our love affair. We couldn't stand to be apart. When we were together, we were constantly touching, swooning, smooching, and staring into each other's eyes. I was almost forty years old, but I felt like a teenager. My body responded to Kyle's in such a physical way: heart fluttering when I saw him, cheeks blushing, tummy warm, my smaller frame drawn into his like a magnet.

This was our first big trip together. My first December break week without the kids. I remember us walking arm in arm through the winding security line, stopping to kiss, hug, and touch. The disgruntled passport officer looked at us and snapped, "Looks like someone's in love."

We didn't need anything external to keep us occupied on the plane. We talked and laughed the whole way. The plastic barrier between our seats felt insurmountable and when the seat belt sign dinged off, I got up and snuggled into his lap.

"You know this stage is going to end, right?" I told him.

He looked at me like I was crazy.

"Don't crush my butterflies," he said. "I'll always have them!"

I hoped he was right, but having fallen in and out of love before, I wasn't optimistic about that early stage lingering. I missed it while I was still in it.

At the resort that week, I alternated between realities. I waffled between the extreme sadness, anguish, and physical pain of being so far from my kids, who felt like an extension of my soul, and elation, electric attraction, and excitement being with Kyle. In meeting and getting to know Kyle, a part of myself that I thought was dead had been resurrected: the fire inside me, what made me *me*. I'd felt like the inside of an old-fashioned barbecue grill long after dinner, a smoking pit of burnt charcoal briquets, white with traces of fire, cracking at the edges, black smoke rising. Done.

Now, suddenly, I was in full blaze, flames flying over the lid of the grill, dancing in the dark. Alive again. And yet, torn apart from the loves of my life for a week that felt endless. I would cry at random times, moon over pictures of them, and mourn as I felt the rope connecting me to them pulling and pulling. It felt familiar, like grief, an emotion I was all too familiar with. But then I would shape-shift into a sex-obsessed adolescent, as I got to know my new love.

That night making s'mores, I'd raced over to the resort's firepit when I saw the crowd forming. I was there simply because I loved s'mores and wanted to make them for myself, not to help my kids make their own. I was ready to feed my starved soul in every way.

Kyle and I were laughing and flirting as we roasted the puffy white confections. An exhausted, downcast mother lording over her sugar-packed kids on the other side of the firepit, looked at us, sighed, and said, "What I wouldn't give for just one minute of that feeling again."

"No, no, no, I was just like you!"

I think about that mother every day.

On so many days, I am her. For so long, I was her. I had lost hope. I had resigned those emotions to the past, stuck in 24/7 parenthood. But then, suddenly, I wasn't.

"I have four kids!" I told her. "I felt the same way. But it can happen! It can."

She shook her head, resigned to her fate. We kept chatting over the fire, my new self confronted with a version of my old self. I touched her arm and smiled as I walked away. I watched her with her family over the next week, waving as we crossed paths.

It has been years since that trip. Everything has changed. Puerto Rico was crushed by a massive hurricane. I'm ensconced in my home with my kids and Kyle. The butterflies still flutter around us, but they've been tempered by world events, stresses, ups and downs, losses, divorces, illnesses.

One summer night, as I was racing around upstairs, exhausted, folding and putting away laundry, trying to get my two teenagers and two little guys to bed, managing work, emails, schedules, books to read, I glanced out back and saw Kyle and a friend of ours outside roasting marshmallows. We have an outdoor fireplace that came with our home, one of the main selling points that I somehow never make time to use. I felt a stab of longing. Had I become the exhausted mom again?

As I put away tiny tank tops inside my daughter's closet, Kyle came bounding in, proudly offering up a s'more he had perfected, made just for me.

I couldn't even eat it.

"Thanks, love, but not now," I said, sighing, harried, stressed, tired.

"But I made it perfectly, just the way you like it!" he said.

I shook my head.

"I just can't right now. I'm trying to get the kids to bed, no one's asleep, it's late. . . ."

He walked out, dejected, taking the s'more with him.

I immediately regretted how I'd handled it. Why hadn't I let myself enjoy the s'more? Why couldn't I have stopped the chaos for a minute and let my own needs be met? Why hadn't I let my husband make me happy, something that would have made *him* feel satisfied and proud? Why did I have to make mothering and housework such an albatross around my neck, something that precluded my own joy?

I found the s'more on my bedside table later that night and climbed into bed, leaving it beside me uneaten. The moment had passed. The s'more had hardened. It sat there all night as the two of us slept.

I miss those butterflies.

I know *I'm* the one who doesn't always stop to see them. But I know they're there, dancing in the dark.

13

I Risked My Life Getting to Curriculum Night on Time

I took home an unexpected lesson from my daughter's Curriculum Night: My compulsion to be absolutely everywhere for each of my kids—and on time—could kill me.

I had left my apartment with plenty of time, but it was UN week in New York and the president was in town. Aggravated, as most New Yorkers are knowing that the city grinds to a halt during the conference, I left twice as much time as I needed to get across town. My then six-year-old had been telling me all about her puppet show video presentation for days. She couldn't wait for me to see it.

As I kissed her goodbye that evening to head back to her school, she reminded me proudly, "Don't forget to listen for my part in the puppet show!"

"Of course! I wouldn't miss it!"

Thirty minutes later, I still hadn't even crossed Central Park. The presentation was starting soon. I had debated getting out of the car and walking for a while, but traffic had been inching forward enough that I still thought I could make it. But now? Not a chance. I was freaking out. I couldn't be late! What if I missed the puppet video?

"I can't miss this!" I exclaimed, frantic.

"Then you better run," my driver said.

Run?

I was wearing the same outfit I'd worn earlier that day to host a forty-person book event: a long wool skirt, a navy-and-tan striped sweater, hoop earrings. Yes, I'd jogged three and a half miles the previous weekend, but I'd done so at such a slow pace that elderly power walkers had whizzed by me—and I'd been in workout clothes.

I opened the car door and burst out, my tote unzipped, and promptly dropped a twenty-dollar bill on the street, only to have a kind gentleman tap me on the shoulder to return it. Instead of wending my way through the beautiful tree-lined paths of Central Park, I decided it would save time if I headed onto the cars-only transverse at 97th Street. As a native New Yorker, I'd driven through crosstown transverses a zillion times, but I'd never walked—let alone run—through any of them.

Now I know why: It's scary. Cars driving east were zooming so close I could feel my skirt swishing. Horns blared. Brakes squealed. No one else was on the sidewalk except for one pack of teenagers who had just finished playing basketball. I ran as fast as I could. Part of me knew this was a bad idea, but there was no turning back.

Midway through the dash, as I started getting tired and winded, I noticed that cars headed west were finally being allowed through the park. If I could just flag down a car and hop in, I could get out of the transverse quicker. My body, more accustomed to a leisurely thirty-minute stroll, was slowing down. But the puppet show! *Gah!* Suddenly, headlights were two inches from my face and multiple horns were honking at me. Holy crap. What was I thinking? I was attempting to *hitchhike*—in the *transverse*? And I'd almost gotten hit.

"Okay, okay!" I said out loud. I tried to take in big, gulping breaths. I mean, come on. I couldn't make it through a measly twelve-minute sprint?

By the time I got to the school, I could barely speak. The Lower School principal greeted me at the door and said gently, "It's okay! Don't rush! It's just starting now!" I raced up the stairs and plopped down into a tiny wooden chair, smushed in between two other parents. Somehow, I was still there in time to introduce myself.

But then I started coughing. At first, it felt like pieces of dust were stuck to the back of my throat. I got up to take a sip of water, but it didn't help. The dust wouldn't go away.

"Now I'm going to show you the puppet video your kids have been working so hard on," the teacher said proudly.

I couldn't breathe. I kept coughing.

"Are you okay?" a mom friend asked, concerned. I coughed and nodded.

Then I thought, *Wait, am I okay? Do I have a cough or is my throat closing up?* Sometimes my body has an allergic reaction when I run. I've repeatedly broken out in hives. An evening sprint is perhaps not what the allergist ordered.

It was getting harder to breathe, but I didn't want anyone to notice. As I watched the puppet video, victoriously catching my daughter's cameo, I started doing mental calculations. Could I get to my preferred hospital in time with all the UN traffic? Did I have an EpiPen with me? Would the school nurse be working this late? How long would I have if my throat *was* closing up? Would an ambulance be able to reach me? What if I made the wrong decision . . . and died?

My friend handed me a Poland Spring bottle. I drank the whole thing, slowly, and tried to calm down.

Please don't close up, please don't close up, I told my throat. Was I getting worse? Better? The same? I tried to sit motionless and inconspicuous, but inside I was panicking.

Was this the end? If so, what a terrible way to go! I could see the headlines: MOM DIES TRYING TO GET TO CURRICULUM NIGHT ON TIME! The articles would talk about the unnecessary pressure moms put on themselves; how hard it was to juggle kids, work, and life; how many mandatory parent events there were these days.

Meanwhile, other parents sauntered in throughout the presentation with slight nods to the teacher, not stressed at all about being late. One dad arrived five minutes before it ended with a smile on his face. *Seriously?* Fortunately, my airways were starting to open.

After the presentation, I told another friend what had happened.

"Wow, I was almost an hour late, but it's my third child so I honestly didn't even worry about it. I'm surprised you did," she said.

Well, it didn't matter that it was my third kid. It could've been my eighteenth kid; it was *that* kid's big night, and I didn't want to let her down. I didn't want to miss something (anything!) she cared about. I wanted to be the perfect parent to *her.* And, I realized, I wanted it so badly that I was willing to put myself in harm's way to achieve it.

I've tried to hold onto the important lesson from that day: I simply have to pick my battles to survive. I have to be okay with being late sometimes. I have to acknowledge that some things are out of my control and that being a "perfect" mom is unrealistic and unattainable. I could have calmly explained to my daughter that things happen despite our best intentions. Perhaps she would have learned the lesson early that I'm just learning now.

But let's be honest. What I really learned was that from now on, I'm wearing a sports bra during UN week.

(Note: After writing a version of this essay, I sent it around to the parents in the class. One of the moms, Vern, stopped me the next day. "You know," she said, "my office at Gersh is right next to a great literary agent. Do you want me to introduce you to Joe Veltre?" I met with Joe in his corner office at Gersh, where he took me on as a client. Joe and I have now sold multiple books and a TV show together. Maybe the running wasn't such a bad idea after all.)

14

My Boys

I'm in bed with three guys, but the only one I'm not touching is my husband. Somehow a pillow has wedged between the two of us, creating a foam wall. I listen to them inhale, exhale. I watch the ceiling as three square shadows with prison-like stripes creep across. It's the middle of the night, but a horn blares. A dog barks. I wonder: *Who is walking their dog at 3:07 a.m.?*

One of the guys I'm snuggling with is a puppy, Yodi, who resembles a stuffed animal. We hosted Yodi for a short while before our babysitter Jamie adopted him. We got him from a friend's breeder in Serbia. He came in a crate with a translation card for the commands he knew in Serbian. We picked him up at the cargo terminal at JFK, already in love.

When I take Yodi for walks, he's attacked by strangers as if he's a Kardashian in Vegas and takes it like a media-trained champ. He is currently nestled in the bend of my knees, getting his beauty rest.

Also in bed is my four-year-old son. His days in this adorable-boy phase are numbered, so I'm inhaling them frantically like a drug that's about to be snatched from my hands. He's my fourth child, so I have the benefit of knowing how fast this will happen. One day I won't be able to lift him. One day, he'll ignore me at a school event—like my older son did recently—and tell me to stop taking so many pictures.

I won't take it personally, I tell myself. But my heart cracks like ice. I can hear it—the cube dunked in a glass of chilled soda. *Crack.*

So when my little guy sneaks into my bed, he stays. I hold his hand and stroke his soft, smooth cheek, watch his eyelids flutter in the dark. I feel his angelic arms around my neck. I take him in, savoring it, grasping onto him.

I know I'll be tired tomorrow; I know I won't fall back asleep. My thoughts will turn to everything I have to do, and then they'll keep turning and turning. But I can't miss this. This joyous, intimate moment with my boy who will be a teenager before I know it.

My custody schedule intensifies my gratitude for these moments. The perspective it affords me is priceless: like a car momentarily protected by an overpass in a rainstorm, the noise stops for just long enough for me to register the silence before the pounding resumes. I can step back a bit. Process. Be grateful.

I had a moment earlier this week, the day before I got the kids back, when I found myself walking alone down Madison

Avenue. I'm hardly ever alone. I left my phone jostling in the bottom of my purse and headed purposefully toward William Greenberg Desserts to pick up the "special snack" for my daughter's class party the next day. No matter whose "day" it is, I'm always the mom.

Everyone I passed along the way triggered something in me. Two ponytailed, makeup-free mom friends with telltale bags under their eyes pushed strollers side by side. I scooted around them and remembered that stage with a pang of nostalgia, but also with relief that it wasn't my life anymore. I turned sideways to get past two elderly women, slowly clanking walkers, and their aides. Will that be me? I passed moms my age with kids freshly picked up from school: my tribe. I greeted the ones I recognized with a warm smile.

I want my kids. I want to be picking them up and rushing to doctor's appointments and gymnastics practice. Even though I'll be doing that tomorrow, it doesn't fill the void today.

In New York, these intimate, everyday moments are all out in the open. All sorts of relationships are on the sidewalk stage. A mom walks comfortably alongside her towering teenage son, looking up at him. He stares straight ahead as he speaks. Will that be my younger son and me?

I see evidence of the passage of time everywhere. I get a preview of being an empty-nester wandering around the city. This is part of the reason I like to flee to LA when I don't have the kids. There, everything occurs in private—in cars, homes, and clubs. I can drive around happily, avoiding school car pool lines, playgrounds, and other places that make me miss my brood. Here in New York, however, it's unavoidable. Life's thrum is a daily assault. I feel like I need to race against the clock if I want to experience everything before time's up.

I cling a bit tighter to my little boy in the dark, knowing how soon I'll be letting him go. I stroke Yodi's soft furry ears. I listen to the comforting sound of Kyle sleeping, knowing that, God willing, he'll be by my side for whatever life throws at us until the end. And I lie there, watching the shadows dance on the ceiling, savoring this moment in bed with my boys.

15

Our Own Memorial This Memorial Day

"Mom! Why is there still salt and pepper in the salt-and-pepper shakers?"

My six-year-old son is holding two ceramic bunnies that we've extricated from thick white packing paper. He tips them over again, just to confirm that the familiar flecks are indeed spilling out onto the carpet. He laughs, incredulous.

"Stop," I say gently, reaching out for his soft hands.

We're down in the basement. Heavy rain, relentless for two days straight, pounds the roof overhead, the pitter-patter of splatter the soundtrack of our soppy Memorial Day weekend.

An hour earlier, he'd snuggled beside me while I was cozy, reading on the couch, and asked if we could finally unpack Treats's and Nene's boxes, the ones that had been standing sentry in our guest room downstairs since last September. The boxes contained everything from Susan Felice Owens ("Treats") and Marie Felice ("Nene"), Kyle's mom and grandmother.

They'd been living together in Charlotte, North Carolina, when they'd both caught Covid and died six weeks apart.

"Can we, Mom? Let's make it into a real room so their souls can come visit," he said. I set my book down.

Once Kyle and his sister, Stefanie, gave us the okay, we got started.

Now we are standing among towering boxes filled with the artifacts of two lives. As we soon discover, more than two lives. Mixed in with the everyday stuff of Treats's and Nene's days, like their bedside clocks, notepads, screwdrivers, pot holders, and hand soaps, are archives of more ghosts. Kyle's late grandfather's belongings, including newspapers saved from the Normandy invasion, his stamp collection, and an American flag, are folded neatly in a plastic container. Two of their late dogs' ashes are in small, cherrywood boxes, each with a picture of the beloved canine on top. When I unwrap those, I have to stop and run to the bathroom to wash away the dust from my hands.

What had been a place for the kids to play hide-and-seek over the past season is slowly turning into what looks like a yard sale. Or, perhaps, Party City. Clearly, Treats and Nene knew how to celebrate life. Three boxes of Christmas ornaments and a knee-high Santa mingle with a bevy of Easter bunnies, a squat, hand-painted Halloween pumpkin, and Thanksgiving turkeys. Celebration overtook function in what they saved, reflecting their joie de vivre.

My son tips the saltshaker over again, a glint in his eye. "Mom, why?"

I take a deep breath.

"Well, love, when you die, you don't know you're about to die. It happens suddenly. One minute you're alive and then the next minute, you're not. You don't usually have time to empty out your salt-and-pepper shakers."

He nods, satisfied with my answer. "Are you about to die?"

"No, I'm healthy. I'm young. I'm not going to die anytime soon. Don't worry. Now go add these to the fragile pile."

He walks toward the window, a bunny in each hand.

I feel like a liar. I can't guarantee my lifespan. No one can. I could get hit by a bus that afternoon. I could have a heart attack. Anything could happen. My own first experience with Covid knocked me into bed for a week. What if I hadn't survived? The average lifespan statistics mean nothing when mixed in with the randomness of life. But how can I explain that? A child feeling like his mom's life—and his own—could end at any minute would make it impossible to sleep at night.

Years later, I will sit on his bed in the dark as he says, "It's not fair. I'm the youngest and you're already old. I won't get as much time with you as everyone else." My heart breaks. Later still he'll say, looking wistfully at our family, "One day, there will only be one of us left." I'll try to console him, cheerfully saying, "Maybe not! Maybe we'll all die together!" But that does little to quell his fear of being the last one standing of our brood. Unthinkable.

We continue unpacking. Unwrapping. I am a Tasmanian devil in pajamas, plowing through each box. I must finish. I must keep going. I pull out purse after purse, making a pile next to the bed, but then as I extract a heavier one from the box, I pause. I can feel its heft and hear its telltale jangles before I see its contents. I peer reluctantly inside. It's the purse that Treats must have been carrying as she went to the hospital to say goodbye to her mother. A wallet. Scrunched-up tissues. A mask and plastic gloves. Her mother's reading glasses with a Covid positive tag dangling off the side. Cough drops. A lipstick. Sunglasses. A half-empty pack of gum. Loose coins.

"Mom, are you going to cry?" my little one asks, suddenly beside me and scanning my eyes for clues. He can read my emotions like they're posted on a billboard. "Did you know when other people start crying, it makes me cry, too?"

"Me too," I say. "I'm okay. I'm just a little sad."

He hugs me around my waist. We stand like that for a while, amid the ancient photo albums, the horse ribbons, the 1980s Broncos baseball hats, the piles and piles of Treats's shoes (who knew?), the half-rinsed pans, the toaster with the crumbs spilling out, the hamper with clothes still in it.

Life, interrupted.

Frozen forever at a random moment in time.

The stuff of life is, of course, just stuff. What matters in the end are the memories from photos, the handwritten recipes, the birthday cards with meaningful notes, the mementos. Not the shoes, although they were pretty fabulous.

By nightfall, we finish our job. All the objects are freed from hibernation, out in the air again. I call out to my son, now playing with a friend in the next room.

"It's all done! Come see!"

His eyes light up in excitement. "The room is ready?"

He runs in. He rarely walks. He scans the room. The window ledge overflows with figurines. Mugs, plates, and vases cover the floor. Books tower high in a corner. Kitchen gadgets rest next to framed photos. Dog beds. Hand-knitted, multicolored blankets. Holiday ornaments. Measuring cups.

He smiles and walks around carefully, silently, through the belongings. Then, he looks up at me and nods.

"Now we can play."

16

Why I "Write" Anthologies

"What even *is* an anthology?" my younger son asked at the dinner table as I talked about *Moms Don't Have Time to Have Kids.*

"It's a collection of essays written by lots of different people," I said.

He looked pensive.

"So then why do you say you wrote it?"

He had a point there.

Before I edited my first anthology, *Moms Don't Have Time To: A Quarantine Anthology*, I'd gotten consistent advice from people I knew in the literary world: Steer clear of anthologies. Why? Apparently, they were too much work. Too hard. Too many contracts. Too many people to deal with.

I remember thinking that hard work had *never* scared me and that a few contracts seemed like a small price to pay for a fabulous collection of essays. I'd loved reading many anthologies over the years, like *The Bitch in the House*, edited by Cathi Hanauer; *Modern Love*, edited by Daniel Jones; *Well-Read Black Girl*, edited by Glory Edim; and, more recently, *On Being 40(ish)*, edited by Lindsey Mead. Why not try?

My first anthology was a bit of a fluke. I'd published many mid-pandemic essays (with contracts!) on my website, so I easily turned those into a book. My second anthology was more traditional: I had to assign the essays and collect them in a meaningful way. From scratch.

Planning an anthology is like hosting an amazing party. The key to its success is inviting the right combination of guests. Everyone has to bring something a little different to the table. My job is to welcome them at the door with a warm smile and a cool drink.

Reading the essay submissions gave me the chills. When Lily King, bestselling author of *Writers & Lovers* and, later, *Heart the Lover,* emailed me her essay, I giddily opened the Word doc named "For Zibby." From Lily King! Her story was a deep, heartfelt meditation on the health struggles she was having with her daughter. Personal. Poignant. Beautifully written. The backstory I never would have known.

Submitting an essay to an anthology is like handing over a child to a babysitter. It's your baby, but you trust someone to take good care of it. I always did love babysitting. As the book neared its publication date, I sent group emails to the literary giants. They've become a team to me, a group, a community. So much of the writing life is solitary. Assembling authors for an anthology, a shared purpose, is rewarding for me as the curator, yes, but also, hopefully, for the contributors. And it hasn't been that hard. Writing my own memoir was about one trillion times harder.

I'm glad I didn't listen to the experts. My (now) three anthologies have brought me enormous joy and a true sense of community. My email group chat with the contributors to *On Being Jewish Now* is still going strong as we celebrate the collection being on the *USA Today* bestseller list for twenty-nine weeks. For each book, I've introduced authors to each other and facilitated new friendships. Recently, two contributors posted about how they'd met through me and had gone on to do book events together. Other contributors have posted from dinner parties. These micro-communities lead to more conversations, events, and collaborations. It makes me smile seeing photos on social media of authors I've connected, out and about. The books have also inspired more communal gatherings all over the country as different combinations of contributors set out to spread the word.

So why do I "write" them? Because the sum of the parts is greater than the whole. Because aggregating diverse voices and perspectives is the key to empathy. Because I like to know the innermost thoughts of the outermost authors. Because just like after a great party, I like going to bed feeling happy, entertained, and delighted by an assortment of interesting people.

Hard work? Bring it on.

17

The Secrets of Divorce Pain

I dropped off the kids in an airport hotel parking lot to spend two weeks with their dad, the longest we would ever be apart. As their little hands waved through the tinted windows, their faces masked by the darkness, I waved back, raising my hand high in the air, a smile on my face.

As soon as the van turned the corner, I collapsed. My legs grew as heavy as tree trunks, my head toppled forward, and I started wailing. I bent over as if my spine had been plucked through the top of my head, rendering me a rag doll. It was a wretched, guttural cry from a place deep inside me, the place filled with all my love for the kids, an untapped reservoir overflowing with feeling. And like feeling the pain of a nerve being zinged, I howled.

I have a history of depression that started in earnest when I was fourteen years old. I went through a period of deep sadness, self-harm, and self-medicating with alcohol. High-functioning depression looks different. I can often pass as fine. I can wipe the tears from my face and do an interview. But not always. It took years for me to find the right combination of meds. Going off Zoloft for my pregnancies and nursing wreaked emotional havoc. It got so bad that during the day, while my big kids were in school and the baby was napping, I would crawl into bed and cry myself to sleep. Once I woke up, I'd count down the hours until I could go to bed again. I didn't want to go out or do anything that would prolong my day. I had no energy. I worried about things constantly.

The thought of a lifetime of bath times and bedtimes, figuring out what to serve for dinner, and coordinating playdates seemed unbearably oppressive, like jumping into a pool wearing a backpack. Some Saturdays, midmorning, I would look at my watch and think, "How am I ever going to make it to bedtime?"

In the evenings, after struggling for hours to keep up appearances—doling out the right amount of discipline and comfort to the kids, managing the anxious thoughts circulating madly in my brain—I would fight back tears reading to the kids. I taught myself a trick: If I counted how many letters were in each word as I read it aloud, I could distract myself just enough to keep from crying. But as the Berenstain Bears and their sunny dirt road whizzed by, the tears would start again.

"Mommy! Stop!" my son would beg as I wiped my eyes.

"I'm so sorry," I'd say, feeling powerless to do so.

One day, while shopping for a kid's birthday gift, I saw a particularly appealing stuffed animal that I thought might cheer *me* up. I bought it. For myself.

When my son, the stuffed animal aficionado, saw it at home, he grabbed it and snuggled it tightly.

"Is this for me?"

"No, sweetie," I said, choking up. "You know how sometimes everybody gets sad? Well, I was feeling blue inside today, so I bought this guy to cheer me up and help me stop crying."

He looked at me quizzically as I wiped my eyes and quipped, "It doesn't look like it's working."

The worst part, truly, during these particularly bleak months, was that nothing was "wrong." I was leading a blessed, privileged life with a healthy family. I had so much to be happy about and nothing that *should* be causing me to be this upset. I knew that and it just made everything worse. How could I be crying in my beautiful bedroom with natural light streaming in midday, when my healthy baby was asleep upstairs and my kids were at great schools?

"But you seem so happy!"

I wasn't.

I finally went back on Zoloft when I finished nursing my baby. I kept waiting for something to change. The blanket was still smothering me. I was starting to despair. Maybe I needed a higher dose? And then one afternoon, I realized I felt just a little better. Lighter. The next day, even more so. I started to notice that I wasn't counting down to bedtime. I was laughing more. When other people got in bad moods around me, I didn't let them drag me down into a vortex. I stayed calm. I didn't engage in fights. I *wanted* to get out of bed.

Within a month, I felt like I was living in a new, easy, effortless world. All that time and energy I'd been spending fighting my depression was suddenly gone. There was a spring to my step. I started having a million creative ideas, like I used to when I was feeling "me." I wanted to start a new business, launch a new nonprofit, write a children's book. I didn't want to go to bed at night; I wanted to watch silly TV shows. I was playful and creative with the kids. When they had tantrums, I didn't. I dealt with problems better. Sure, things still bothered me occasionally, but they didn't throw me off. A sleepless night just left me feeling tired, not unable to function. I couldn't wait to simply live. The thought of a lifetime of figuring out dinner for the kids didn't fill me with dread; it just was.

Sometimes, even now, the pain exceeds what Zoloft can offset, and the dam it has built around my emotions gets knocked down. I succumb to the darkness. I've had to cancel events when I get triggered into this state. Eventually I get out of it, but the separation from the kids occasionally pulls me back in.

This time, at the airport, I logically knew it would be okay. The kids would be totally fine, happy with their dad, whom they loved so much. But oh, the crushing pain of the actual separation.

Kyle lifted me off the ground and led me back to our car. We got lost leaving the hotel, heading south instead of north. I didn't care. I didn't care where we went or how long it took to get home. I didn't want to get home. I didn't want to look around our home in the Palisades, where we'd all just spent two fabulous weeks together filled with laughter, and feel their absence.

The pain took on a physical form. It stretched from my neck down to my C-section scar, where all the kids emerged at one point or another. Usually after I say goodbye every other week, I cry for a bit and then can collect myself. But this time, I couldn't. The forgotten bathing suits, the empty soccer nets in the backyard, and the snacks still on the counter haunted me.

The worst part about divorce pain is that it can feel self-inflicted. Unlike a serious illness that comes on suddenly or a catastrophic accident, the emotional amputation of saying goodbye to kids due to shared custody does have a source. A cause. And in most cases, you, the parent, have played a role in it. That's the hardest part. What if you'd been able to make your marriage work? Why couldn't you? Is anything really that bad, bad enough for this excruciating pain?

Back at home, I hid under the covers.

"Why don't you read, honey?" Kyle suggested, knowing how much I loved it.

For years when the kids were little, I'd felt discouraged and pathetic when it came to reading. The only time I could find to read was when I finally crawled under my covers at night. It would take months for me to get through even a short, mindless story. Most evenings I'd have to backtrack a few pages because I couldn't even remember what I'd read the night before. Short chapters were my savior. I used to stare longingly at the new releases through bookstore windows while pushing my double stroller down the street.

Maybe on vacation, I'd think, sighing.

Now, I had too much time.

I opened the cabinet to look through the books I would feature soon on my podcast. Was there something funny that could take my mind off everything? A thriller, perhaps?

Something amazing? I grabbed *Malibu Rising* by Taylor Jenkins Reid, which many of my trusted reader friends had said kept their interest. I climbed into bed and started reading but decided to download the audiobook instead. I just couldn't focus on the letters. Listening, I fell into the lives of the Riva family, surfing on my belly with them, hating their dad for all his flaws, loving their mom, wiping the sand from my feet, eating the sandwich at the roadside restaurant, prepping for a party. Until I passed out.

"I made us a dinner reservation!" Kyle called from the other room hours later.

"Oh, honey, I can't," I said. "I can't eat. I can't get out of bed."

I didn't want to open my eyes. If I opened my eyes, the pain would come flooding back. And why would I? What was there to see? My work, which typically felt so important, pressing, and fun, faded away into the background. I couldn't possibly email. I couldn't even respond to helpful comments coming in from my Instagram post, a Hail Mary I'd thrown to see if anyone else "out there" felt like me. I was too wrecked to read or respond. I couldn't move.

Kyle climbed in beside me and we looked at all 800-plus pictures from the previous weeks with the kids as the sky blackened. Finally, I was laughing, watching the kids' funny videos, the selfies I didn't know they'd taken.

I've experienced this specific grief in one way or another for years. The feast or famine of shared custody. Time away from the kids stretches out like the snap of a towel at the beach, settling down on the sand for me to traverse one wobbly step at a time. People rarely discuss divorce pain. But the pain is real.

"Want to go in the pool?" Kyle asked the next morning.

I shook my head, remembering all the fun times we'd just had swimming with the kids.

A friend texted me. Did I have a minute to chat?

I called her back right away. She was sobbing.

"I just left my kids with my ex and it hurts so badly. I don't know anyone else who would understand except you. I feel so terrible because I *chose* this. Was it worth it?"

I said everything to her that I needed to hear myself. That it wasn't an option. That the kids would all be okay. That it would get easier the next morning. That the pain was part of the happiness to come. That she was starting fresh and building new memories. And that the feelings were real and raw and justified. Then I told her to put on her prettiest outfit, grab her laptop, and get out of the house. Because, like me, I knew she could turn it on and pretend to be okay in public. And sometimes, just like studies show, if you smile, you actually feel happier. Being out and chatting dulls the pain.

Shared custody, literally losing control legally and physically of all your kids at once, is oppressively awful. And it is a loss. One that deserves space at the crowded dinner table of painful things. Let's give it a seat. Let's name "divorce pain" and come up with greeting cards to address it.

Sorry for your divorce pain. Thinking of you.

Divorce pain? Your table is waiting. Let me show you the way.

Zoloft, please join us.

18

Don't Miss Your Connection

An old, dear friend called me from drop-off. She'd been going through something complicated and, for various reasons, the mom friends in her orbit hadn't been supportive.

"I feel terrible," she said, kids screaming, horns blaring in the background. "I'm dealing with so much, like my kids and their issues; my job, which is going well, but I feel guilty about being away from the kids; everything. And I just feel so alone."

"You are *not* alone," I told her. "Sometimes the people you're with physically aren't your people."

Until I started my podcast and began regularly connecting with like-minded people all over the world, I'd assumed that friends were simply a product of geography. Full stop. Growing up, I made friends from school, sports, or after-school activities. In college, girls from the same dorm. In business school, the same section. In life, the same job or, perhaps, the wider social scene. In mom-life, from the kids' classes. The neighborhood.

And I thought that was it. That was the menu. I could pick and choose the women and men I connected with from that preselected group. Otherwise, the kitchen was closed. Luckily, I've made some amazing lifelong friends that way, friends I rarely see but whom I adore nonetheless. Friends who have moved away but have stayed lodged in my heart forever.

But if I've learned anything from post-pandemic Zoom life, it's that I can get my emotional friendship needs met by firing up my laptop. It's not the same as a walk in the park together or a coffee date where I can physically reach out and hug a friend if she cries. But it's close.

When I started chatting intimately with authors about their books and their lives, I felt that sparkly sisterhood sensation happening often. The children's book author in Nigeria. The journalist in Denmark. The sex expert in London. The Boston-based novelist. The memoirist in China.

I found myself often saying to podcast guests, "Oh my gosh, we need to have coffee or meet up in real life!" Which, of course, we usually don't. What I really meant was: *How great to have found you! Let's not lose this new connection.*

Was it because we shared a passion for reading and writing? Was it because so many authors had what I thought was my original cocktail of anxiety on the rocks with a shot of depression on the side? Or perhaps it was the common instinct of being an observer, of wondering about the people at the next table at a restaurant and inventing stories about them ("maybe that's the au pair and she just had her heart broken and . . ."). Maybe it was because my people, women—and men—who have the same makeup emotionally, also feel the need, the compulsion, to write and to make sense of the world through fingertips on keys.

Not every podcast I record results in a deep connection, that crackling sense of discovery. But many do. It's intoxicating. Perhaps that's why I continue to book so many podcasts each week even when few listeners can keep up.

When concerned colleagues and friends suggest I slow down, I'm like: *No way!* I wish I could do *more.* I fit in as many interviews as I can physically prep for, because what if the author is one of *my people* and I miss my connection?

I used to think terms like "energy work" and "force field" and "spirit" were woo-woo. Now, I'm so in tune with my energy that I reference it like it's my fifth child. I can feel, physically, when someone isn't nice. I sense a rush of cold wind. My body goes on high alert. My posture shifts. Their energy is toxic. Likewise, I can sense someone's generous spirit seeping into my soul like a sip of hot chocolate on a rainy day. It's like I'm one of those Care Bears with light shining from my chest. I can turn on my sensor by flipping an emotional switch.

My default is to assume everyone is a decent, nice person. But I reluctantly recognize that some people simply aren't. They don't root for others. They snap at strangers. They think ambition means achieving at the expense of someone else, that for them to rise up, others have to be squashed down. This is counter to everything I believe. I think the best feeling is when I help someone succeed. That, to me, is real achievement. So I turn on my sensor to see who I'm dealing with.

And I keep hoping that the good in everyone will shine through.

"Seriously," I told my friend on the phone, "your people aren't where you are. And that's okay. Because they're out there. If the women in your class aren't being supportive, smile, be nice and polite, and know that you can pick up the phone and call me anytime. Your people are out there. I promise."

"Thank you," she said. "I feel like no one gets me here, you know? And sometimes that makes me feel nuts."

"I get it," I said. "But you're amazing. Some people *can't* root for others. They're too unhappy themselves or insecure or whatever. They're the ones missing out. We should feel bad for them because they're going through life angry or miserable. But their darkness shouldn't cast such a shadow that it puts out your bright light. Sometimes you have to move out of the way."

"Yeah, maybe you're right." We hung up as she rushed off.

It took me forty-plus years to realize that proximity is just one element of friendship. Real friends who beam out that warm light of connection are everywhere, waiting to be discovered.

It's like there was once a child, sitting cross-legged and playing up in the clouds, putting together a giant, intricate, magic puzzle of a zillion pieces. Once he finished, every piece in the puzzle glowed with a bright light. But then the child took the puzzle apart and, from his perch in the sky, scattered the glowing pieces all over the world, lodging their way into people's souls. Now, whenever any puzzle pieces come close to each other, they know they belong to the same puzzle. They start to glow again. It's up to all of us to find the other pieces. They're out there. Scattered among everyone else, disguised behind various exteriors: different colors, shapes, and sizes masking the simplicity of our shared secret slice.

Hokey? Yes.

True? Absolutely.

19

Saving Time

When I was in fifth grade at my all-girls school, we were assigned Secret Santas. I got a girl named Abigail. We weren't friends, but I was determined to be the best Secret Santa *ever.* I don't remember the actual gifts I made or bought. What I remember is sitting in my closet late at night, surrounded by wrapping paper and bows, markers and tape, and pouring my heart into her gifts.

My mom stood in the doorway of my closet in her floor-length nightgown and terry-cloth bathrobe, a cigarette in her hand, her forehead furrowed, as I sat on the carpet, wrapping.

"Oh, Zib," she said. "I'm worried about how much time and effort you're putting into this."

"Why?" I asked, confused.

"Well, I just don't know if *your* Secret Santa will be doing this for you. And I don't want you to be disappointed with the gifts *you* get."

That moment feels like yesterday. Me, on the floor looking up at my mom. Her staring down at me. The wrapping paper strewn all about. Her words and the smoke hanging in the air between us.

"But, Mom," I said, "that's not what it's about. I don't even care what I get. I want to make *my* Secret Santa happy. I *like* doing this."

When online shopping came on the scene, I breathed a sigh of relief. Phew! *This* would make things easier. No more going from store to store. No more browsing or waiting in line. I was an enthusiastic early adopter. For the past few years, I've found myself doing all my holiday shopping late at night from bed, but it has been an unwelcome obligation, one that came out of my reading time and from which I derived no pleasure.

Fast-forward to "adding to cart." Where was the joy in that? Online shopping may have saved me some time, which I'm always desperate for, but it was robbing me of pleasure. Worst of all, it wasn't letting my kids see how much joy there was in gift giving. The excitement of finding just the right thing. Then, the crinkling of wrapping paper. The hunt for scissors. The stack of crisp new packages with handwritten notes.

One year, I gathered my kids and had them make lists of all the people we needed to give presents to. My younger daughter picked a store she thought would be best. She grabbed her scooter, as did my son. They donned helmets, my older daughter changed her phone case, again, and off we went.

The walk itself, dodging strangers, looking in windows, stopping in Starbucks, was filled with laughs. When we got to the store, I assigned each kid one of their cousins and said, "Go!"

My little guy bopped off, dragging his giant shopping cart behind him like Linus's blanket.

"Do you think he'll like this?" he asked, holding up a shirt for his cousin.

"Hmm, maybe," I said. "Keep looking."

"Mom!" my daughter called from the other side. "I think she'll love this tie-dye sweater!"

"Okay! Put it in your cart!"

One by one, we found something special for everyone. We carried out our three giant bags, stopped for a do-it-yourself frozen yogurt, and then spread all our merchandise all over the living room carpet, where we started wrapping all of it.

"Do you think they'll like their gifts?" my little guy asked, nuzzling up next to me.

"I do!" I said. "Do you?"

"Me too."

I stroked his hair as we walked out of the living room, taking a glance back at our hard work.

Sometimes it pays to ask: What am I saving the time *for*?

I'm obsessed with productivity, eyes often on the clock. I get asked frequently how I manage my time. I don't exactly know how I do it, but I know when to save time and when to indulge in time spent with others.

I differentiate between tasks that I have to do alone versus tasks that can be done with the kids around. Anything I can do with them, I do. When I'm not with them, I do work stuff that requires me to close the door, like podcasts and recording ads. I handwrite lists whenever I feel stressed, sometimes allocating the time it'll take and scheduling when I'll do it. I obsessively file my emails: to read; to write; to blurb; to record; pitches by publication month; submissions to evaluate. I plan my reading by my calendar.

Also, I make sure I don't let my inbox get above 300 emails or, at most, 500, before sitting down, alphabetizing by sender and working my way down. When I get overwhelmed, I start from the bottom and work my way up instead. I say no to most social plans. I read quickly and have taught myself how to speed-read. Reading pace isn't fixed for life; it can be sped up like a track and field athlete training for a race.

I don't need that much sleep and catch up when I really need to crash. I make decisions quickly. I make sure to have smart people on my team whom I trust. I can work from anywhere—a doctor's waiting room, an airplane. I do everything *right away* or else I forget. It's faster to do it and get it off my plate before it can settle. I don't belabor emails, essays, newsletters. I just do them.

At home, I don't allow phones at dinner and eat every possible night with Kyle and the kids. I try to schedule all my work travel when they're with their dad. Kyle and I divide house responsibilities. I'm lucky he cooks and deals with our dog most of the time. I only do laundry on the weekends. I don't cook except breakfast, which often involves a microwave. I rarely drive, always opting to be a passenger.

Mostly, I view every day as a new challenge and a chance to do better, even if that means rescheduling flights, changing hotels, or rearranging plans. If there's a better potential outcome, I'll try it. When I'm doing something, I'm 100 percent focused on it. When I'm interviewing someone, that's all I'm thinking about. When I'm selecting books to buy for the bookstore, that's all I'm doing. One thing at a time with hyperfocus, even if it's throwing the football with my son before bed.

It isn't perfect, but it works. My systems help, but I operate at a pretty quick speed. I hum along, super-productive. Occasionally, when a dark mood or loss or illness gets in the way, I get knocked down and think, "Is that how other people feel? I'd never be able to get anything done!" But then it passes and I'm on the work speedway again. I do my best and then move on. I get stressed. Sometimes I cry. And then I try again the next day.

I've learned to grab moments when I can and eke out any productivity whenever possible. When friends ask for advice, here's what I say.

Keep your big goal in sight at all times, but don't try to accomplish it. I always knew that I wanted to write a book. But when I was at home with the kids, I could barely get through reading *Goodnight Moon*, let alone write a novel. Instead, I tended to the fire within me. I kept reading whenever possible, propping up books on my pump, reading in down moments, reading before bed. I thought of funny moments and wrote them down in sentences, in emails, or as scribbles on paper that I tossed in my top desk drawer. I didn't realize it at the time, but that became the research phase. Information gathering. There are a lot of stages to every project. Take notes. Do adjacent things to your goals in the time you have. A sentence isn't a novel, but it sure does feel good to write one.

Take the kids with you. As my kids got older, I would take them to things like local book festivals. I'd introduce them to authors at bookstore story times. I'd make up plots and test them out on the kids. Instead of waiting to find "me time," bring your kids into more activities you might enjoy without them. Share your passions with the kids. Mine was easier because kids also tend to love books. But taking them to a local library for an afternoon made *me* happy, too, and kept me closer to what I wanted to be doing professionally. Don't feel like you need to wait, dress up, and get out to explore your area of interest. Do it together. Go to the places and spaces that make you feel like *you*.

Ask for their advice. I involve the kids as much as possible. "What do you think should happen at the end of the story I'm writing?" "How do you think we can campaign together to win this podcast award?" "What do you think about this book cover?" I often take their advice, which makes them feel great; kids love being respected for who they are and what they think. We think we need to be there to entertain them, but they have a lot of ways to help *us*. There's nothing like seeing the pride on a child's face after they've done something "grown-up" to help you.

Get divorced. I'm kidding. Kind of. Every other weekend, I have time without the kids to sleep, write, read, catch up, and remember who I am. You don't have to get divorced to do this. Take advantage of other people in your life who love your kids and give both them and the kids the gift of time together *without you*. It doesn't mean you're shirking your responsibilities. It means you're offering up an experience to, say, your mom or your partner or your cousin, even your spouse, to bond meaningfully with your little one. Those moments and relationships are key. Leave the kids with your parents or your sister *without guilt.* I wish I'd done that more. Think back on your own childhood: Didn't you love the time you spent with your grandparents? I know I did.

Draw the picture. Instead of laying out paper and crayons for the kids and then grabbing your phone or rushing off to get lunch going, stop and draw. Sit quietly for even a few minutes and do something creative *with* your kid. Compare colors. Get inspiration. It might not be the creativity you're looking for exactly, but any project that draws on your senses and soul will rev your engine. Do the silly things. Engage. Don't miss the opportunities that are literally right in front of you.

Don't be so hard on yourself. I know, I know. I used to read that advice and roll my eyes. But *really.* This is as hard as it gets. Everyone says to "cherish every moment," but just acknowledge that having kids is challenging, even when it's amazing. There may *not* be time today. But there might be tomorrow. Someday, you'll have more time than you know what to do with.

When our extended family exchanged gifts that holiday season, I watched with pride as the kids handed out their thoughtfully selected, hand-wrapped presents. They beamed as they saw how their effort that day had translated into others' happiness.

I could've ordered it all online myself. But oh, what I would've missed.

20

What's Your Sign?

Every day on the way to school, I read my kids their horoscopes. I flip through the *New York Post* as we speed across town until I find the right page and then ask, "Who wants to go first?" Some mornings, the kids leave the car with a kiss goodbye and run into school clutching their backpacks in one hand and the torn-out gray square of their horoscope in the other.

Fast-forward to one summer afternoon when my nephew and I were shopping for my daughter's birthday.

"Oh, this place looks cute," I said, steering us into a shop.

As we plowed through sections devoted to TikTok-inspired cookbooks and ramen-shaped sponges, I came across a game called What's Your Sign? It was the same shape as Cards Against Humanity, clearly a card-based family crowd-pleaser.

"Perfect!" I said out loud.

"Yeah, she'll love that." My nephew approved.

I carried the game around the store, waited in the checkout line, carried it home, gift-wrapped it, and brought it back with me, all without ever reading the fine print.

When my daughter opened it on her birthday morning, her eyes lit up. "What's Your Sign? Like our horoscopes in the car?!" she said.

"Exactly!"

"Aw," she said. "Thanks, Mom!"

I beamed. The satisfaction of a thoughtful gift.

During a driving rainstorm that night, we decided to go out for dinner. I grabbed the game, still on the dining table, and threw it into my tote as we raced to the car. We often play games with the kids during dinner.

We descended on the local high-end burger joint: my kids; Kyle; my brother, Teddy; and my nephew. When the kids started getting a bit restless waiting for the food, I pulled out the game. *Genius move,* I thought, mentally patting myself on the back. *I'm such a good mom. Always prepared.*

The kids switched seats so they could be on one side of the table to play. Teddy, Kyle, and I chitchatted as the kids divvied up the cards. Suddenly, my daughter flashed a card in front of my face and said, "Uh, Mom? What does *this* mean?"

I looked at it.

"You will have an intense orgasm."

Wait, what?

"Mom, look at this one," my son said.

His card read: *"You will have unprotected sex."*

Oh no, oh no, oh no.

"Give me the cards," I said, standing up and frantically trying to grab them away. "Guys! Give me the cards!"

The kids all started laughing, realizing that somehow, they'd gotten their hands on something totally inappropriate. And that I was freaking out. They started reading the cards out loud as I lunged toward all of them.

"You will find yourself in a sticky situation."

I started laughing uncontrollably and saying, "Stop!" as they all threw out words like *humping.*

"Oh my God," I kept saying, laughing so hard that tears rolled down my face. "I can't believe I did this."

"It says seventeen and up!" my daughter said, pointing at the box. "Look!"

She was ten.

"I didn't even *read* the box!" I cried. "I just assumed it was fine!"

I grabbed the game and got up to throw it away. The kids followed me.

"Hey, Mom, what's *anal*?"

"Mom, what's *masturbating*?"

I shook my head, praying that no one was in the other stalls.

"Let's talk about this another time, okay? Please?" I pleaded, shoving the game deep into the ladies' room garbage can.

When we got back to the table, I sat down to hear my brother explaining, ". . . and then you pull it over like a raincoat for a banana."

He paused and looked over at me.

"Thanks, Aunt Zibby."

My older son recently commented, "Have you noticed that a lot of our trips and meals are what you call 'memorable'?" Meaning: disasters.

It's true. My best-laid plans for the kids often backfire. If only my horoscope would warn me.

21

You've Got Mail: Revisited Twenty-Five Years Later

The first time I watched the movie *You've Got Mail* was right after I graduated from college. I was living in West Hollywood, working at a small brand development and design firm in Studio City. My soon-to-be ex-boyfriend, whom I moved to LA to be with, was working an intense job with long hours, so I had a lot of time to myself after work. Free time was new for me and, actually, unwelcome. I'd been an intense student, working relentlessly to graduate from college with honors. Suddenly, the nights seemed to stretch on with no work assigned.

I decided to take a personal essay writing class at the UCLA Extension School. Years later, when I'd drive by with Kyle he'd joke, "Look! Your alma mater!" The only thing I remember producing was a piece about buying my first bra with my mother at Bergdorf's at age nine and hiding between the silk robes so no one would see me. I'd been determined to become a writer since I was young, but I knew there was no direct path there. I'd resolved to take the winding road through life, hoping I could get there, somehow.

You've Got Mail allowed me to luxuriate in the dream life of owning The Shop Around the Corner children's bookstore, which Meg Ryan's character inherited from her beloved late mother. The setting on the Upper West Side was so familiar to me as a lifelong New Yorker that it made me smile and want to call my high school friends on their landline numbers, which I still remembered. Was I in the background somewhere? I ate it all up as I clung to my dream of authordom.

Twenty-five years later, I'm watching *You've Got Mail* on my flight from New York to Los Angeles, on my way to the opening of my own bookstore, Zibby's Bookshop, in Santa Monica.

My bookshop is only 823 square feet, but it is already magical, designed to look like my living room, the shelves curated by topic and emotion, and the store filled with nonstop author events and conversations. The *Los Angeles Times* did a big piece about the store that I reread many times to make sure those kind words were still there in black and white.

Having worked in advertising, psychology, and marketing roles with one short internship at *Vanity Fair*, I didn't know a lot about the publishing industry the first time I watched *You've Got Mail*. This time, I caught all the references. It was like Nora Ephron had written the movie for me. Tom Hanks's girlfriend in the film, played by Parker Posey, was the head of a publishing company. She threw around mentions of the PEN gala and so many other mainstays of the publishing business. The bookstore sales figures she shared sounded like the talk I'd had with my accountant about our projected sales last week.

Soon, we'll land. Soon, the store will open. Soon, my career—all those ups and downs, turbulence, and travel—will have led somewhere definitive. The bookstore to me isn't about commerce. It's about community, building a place that others cherish, that helps readers discover books and authors they never would have otherwise. It's a profound responsibility that I take quite seriously.

So here it comes. The end of the film. The end of the flight. The end of a chapter. The start of another.

The credits are rolling. The next movie is queued up to start.

Here I go.

22

Getting Back on the Horse

I went horseback riding recently for the first time since I was ten years old. Or rather, I went timidly clomping around the ring, the horse held by the instructor, while I watched my daughter trot and post like a pro. As I climbed up the little plastic two-step staircase, my legs were shaking.

"You really think I can do this?" I asked the teacher.

"Yes! Just swing one leg over."

"You got this, Mom," my daughter shouted from across the ring.

With a little yelp, I grabbcd thc horsc's manc plus thc rcins and somehow, inelegantly, righted myself. And wow, was it higher up there than I remembered. Why was I now scared of heights? My shoulders tensed. My knuckles turned white from clutching the reins so tightly. The bike helmet I was wearing—that I'd quickly snatched from a bin in the garage—slipped sideways. All the while, I tried to smile in my daughter's direction, too afraid to take my hands off the reins to give her a thumbs-up.

When the horse started moving, I gasped. Was it always this rocky? I felt like I was on a soon-to-capsize ship. Would I fall off, get a concussion, become paralyzed, or even die? I played out all the terrible outcomes in vivid detail. I do this all the time. Ambulances swirled in my mind, then surgeries, wheelchairs, ramps in my home, and then, my funeral, which I replay often. One therapist said I do this to force myself to live more fully in the present. Evidently, I need a casket to ground me.

On the horse, I was terrified. The fact that I rode for years as a little girl—until my allergies got so bad I had to quit—didn't help. Turns out my muscle memory is as terrible as my actual memory. The only thing I seem to have a permanent capacity for storing away is book plots.

And yet, as I listened to the instructions, walked around the ring, and realized I was okay, I started to relax. My shoulders released from their perch under my ears. My fingers unclenched. By the end of the session, I even trotted in a circle around my teacher for about thirty seconds. It wasn't pretty, but I did it.

Dismounting, I closed my eyes and held my breath, clinging to the saddle for dear life as my body slid down the horse's side. Finally, my feet were back on the dirt. It wasn't until I took a wobbly step forward that I realized my inner thigh muscles were on fire.

"Oh, you're going to be sore in places you didn't even know you had," the teacher cautioned.

"Good job, Mom!" my daughter called out, beaming at me.

"Thanks, love!" I said, beaming back.

I've gotten back on many metaphorical horses lately.

At forty, I decided to upend my life, in part to model for the kids what it meant to be a happy mother, one who could share her voice the same way I wanted them to share theirs. Who knew that after almost a decade, we would really be helping each other?

Life has been rocky as I've navigated new terrain. I've clutched the reins of change for dear life. Ironically, it has been my kids helping me through, just like my daughter did in the ring. They've been cheering me on as I tackle revisions on my novel or when I debate acquiring a new manuscript.

They're the ones who say, "You got this, Mom," when I sigh and stress over my overflowing inbox. They're the ones I think about when I launch a new business line or start a new project.

My daughter and I held hands as we walked back to the car, our helmets swinging in our free hands. We looked at each other and smiled.

Yes, I thought. *We got this.*

23

My Mother's Napkin Holders Mean Summertime and Love

They are painted in a range of blues, reds, and whites, with little black dots for the eyes.

Some are tall and thin while others are shorter, squatter. They aren't too heavy, less than an orange but more than a clementine. I stare down at one of them in the palm of my hand, and what looks like the top of a fin protrudes slightly over my fingertips.

I wouldn't have thought that a set of fish-shaped napkin holders would be the object that most represents my mother and our summers together. But they are. The fish are carved in profile, painted on both sides, with holes in the middle for the napkins, puncturing their stomachs. Do fish have stomachs? These fish live in my mom's home in the Hamptons and have since the 1970s, when we first set down roots there in the middle of the potato fields.

Every family lunch, birthday celebration, dinner party, or

summer barbecue, my mother's table would be set ahead of time. Cornflower blue or white, the napkins would offset the bright, painted, almost tropical design of the wooden holders that would clang together as she cleared them from the table after the meal.

The sight of the napkin holders on display meant the meal was going to be important. This wasn't another tuna salad pita sandwich with celery and carrot sticks on the side. It would be an *occasion*. I should dress properly.

When I was young, my mother would outfit my little brother and me in matching prints before the meals, a barrette in her mouth as she brushed my thick, long, brownish-blond hair into submission to rest just so. Sometimes she traded it for a rubber band and then covered that with a beautiful ribbon that she pulled out of her baggie, her secret stash of ribbons.

At fancier dinner parties to which my brother and I weren't invited, the fish sometimes stayed tucked away in the heavy wooden drawer of the hutch, painted blue and white plates with a couple of small seagull sculptures scattered about the shelves above them. When company came, the nicer silverware appeared, perhaps some silver napkin rings that would sit to the side of the calligraphed place cards. Always place cards.

My mom would often have dishes of chocolate scattered around the table between the blossoming hydrangea arrangements, delivered earlier that day. Sometimes she padded out barefoot into the yard and carefully clipped flowers from the garden.

For those events, we were often paraded out in matching bathrobes, wearing identical red slippers with soft black soles.

A headband rested over my freshly conditioned and combed hair, the green claw-toothed Tangle Tamer having done its work. We were allowed to say hello, and then put to bed early, dozing off while listening to the sound of grown-ups laughing, talking, gossiping without us. Sometimes I would open the door to my small bedroom with the white iron bedframe and lavender quilt and look down the long hallway to see if I could catch a glimpse of the adults, smoke trailing their cigarettes or cigars, ice clinking.

But the fish, those were for us. That meant we kids were welcome. Invited and expected to behave, sit down, napkins on our laps, elbows off the table. We were supposed to compliment my mother on the food whether she'd made it herself or not, particularly her famous cheesecake, a recipe passed down from my grandmother.

Now, when we all pile into the car and drive to my mom's house, I know the fish will be out, as freshly painted as always, swimming along through our seasons.

"Let's play our game," I tell the kids as we drive over. "When you see a napkin in a fish napkin holder, you a) leave it there the whole time; b) pull it out and put it on your lap; or c) grab the whole thing and throw it in the pool."

They all laugh and scream, "B! B!"

Later, at the table, I give the little ones an elbow nudge with a quick glance toward the fish as we sit down. They smile.

"Remember these, Zib?" my mom always says.

"Of course!"

My kids pick the fish up, turn them over in their hands, discard them to the side of their personalized mugs and the white ceramic corn on the cob holders my mom has also had since I was young. Their napkins disobey and slide off their laps, eventually landing under the feet of our dogs, who pad across them, back and forth, hunting for scraps or waiting for my youngest to feed them hamburger buns.

"Mimi is pretty strict," they whisper.

"Shhh!"

At our home, I am much more lenient. My littlest often runs around the table, sometimes even scootering around us. Various kids hide under the table. We all get up and down throughout the meal, which we serve family style. It is loud and chaotic and amazing.

We use cloth napkins only when my mother comes over. She ordered them for me after we had her over for dinner once; they arrived the next day via Amazon. We have them ready when she arrives.

We are often either repeating or resisting how we were raised. I can't maintain my mom's standards. It's a battle I haven't picked with my crew. I embrace the disorder, kids talking over each other, yelling, laughing, and calling out. Sometimes I put my head in my hands at the craziness of it all, but I love it that way. During the pandemic, I would order pizza, slap down the box in the center of the kitchen table without plates, napkins, or silverware, and just say, "Dive in."

My mother is in her seventies and I'm in my forties. I'm all too aware that life is short and that our days are numbered. It isn't my mom's beautiful abstract paintings, fancy silver, designer duds, or intricate jewelry that I'll want.

It's the fish.

24

Lessons from My Dad

My dad and I have always had a super close relationship. When I was a little girl, I couldn't wait for him to come home from work, even if I could only catch a quick glimpse of him as he shaved, donned a tuxedo, and headed out again. I craved nights when he could put me to bed, tuck me in, and tell me a story. I beamed when he spoke to my third grade class about the stock market. As I grew up, I confided in him about my relationships, my fears, my complicated decisions. He has always been there for me, no matter how busy he is. Now, mostly, he accidentally butt-dials me. I smile as the call quickly drops.

Call me on purpose sometime, I text. He calls right away. I've realized that my dad has truly taught me the rules of how to live, work, and love. Here's how.

Find the humor. No matter how stressed my dad gets running his business, he's the first one to stop and make a pun or punctuate a serious conversation with an unexpected animal noise. "I had a meeting with a world leader last week," he'll say. "Hadn't seen him in a dog's age. Woof, woof!" Then he'll erupt into fits of laughter.

Show your kids they're important. In 2007, my dad was on a road show, giving a series of presentations to potential investors, when taking his company public. In a massive New York hotel ballroom, he was at the podium, halfway through one of the most important speeches of his career, when I called from the hospital to announce I'd just had twins. He not only picked up my call but also spoke to me for a minute and then snapped his phone shut and told the thousands of attendees, "Gotta go. My daughter just had twins." And waltzed off the stage.

Always answer the phone. No matter how busy my dad is at work, I know that I can always reach him. His assistants know that if I call, no matter what he's doing or who he's with, he'll always pick up my call. I don't abuse this privilege, typically opting to tell them he can call me back whenever he has time, but knowing that the phone line is always open gives me a sense of comfort and security well into middle age.

Throw yourself into what you love to do. My dad still works nonstop, even now as he approaches eighty. He may not be in the office daily anymore, but he's always reading through a stack of papers, on calls, or deeply connected, thinking. When asked if he'll retire, he looks at the questioner quizzically. "Why would I do that?" For him, a life of relaxation isn't fulfilling. His purpose is to create and innovate, to build and improve. It fuels his every moment.

Only take the sleep you need. My dad goes through the

workweek with only a few hours of sleep each night, catching up on lazy Saturday mornings by sleeping in. He and his brothers simply don't need that much sleep to function optimally. I think I inherited that gene.

Don't give up. When founding his business, my dad approached hundreds of investors for funding, getting painful rejections from trusted colleagues. But he knew he had a good idea and didn't stop until he got what he needed, despite the slog of nos. Same thing when raising money for the Schwarzman Scholars program in China. He listened to his inner compass and stayed the path, creating something amazing.

Read. In my dad's favorite space in his apartment, a giant closet with a couch and TV at the center, he has piles of books scattered on the floor. I have to walk around them to find him on his favorite armchair, careful not to tip over a pile. I don't know when he finds time to read, but he constantly plows through books: history, thrillers, social science, nonfiction. He'll always stop to tell me about a "fascinating" book he has just finished like *Bad Blood* by John Carreyrou. He also reads multiple newspapers from around the world daily.

Have fun. My dad has always loved a good party, whether it's one he's throwing with my stepmother or a costume party for which he goes all out. He stays out late, loves to dance, rarely drinks, and delights in a festive occasion. He's often the last to leave the dance floor.

Trust your gut. Several unsavory figures have tried to get my dad to do business with them. He can sense if something seems off about someone instantly and, even if there's nothing he can put his finger on, extracts himself from the situation.

Don't be afraid of change. My dad often says, "Life's too short to be miserable." If something isn't working, even something huge like, say, a marriage, it's never too late to make a change.

Take care of your body. He views his body like a puzzle, making sure each piece fits with the others. If one piece gets damaged, the whole thing falls apart. He eats well, exercises daily, and says, "I've been thin and I've been heavy. But it seems like being thin is the key to living longer. So, I'm doing that." He walks on the treadmill even though he complains about it and was still playing competitive tennis until recently. He regularly sees doctors and takes care of himself.

"Fuck 'em." At the end of the day, he doesn't care what people think. There will always be doubters who say something can't be done. He just doesn't listen.

Remember that you don't have to be the smartest person in the room. He always says that he isn't that smart and that he isn't even particularly good at math, but he surrounds himself with people far smarter than he is.

Appreciate beauty. The view of the ocean. A sunset. A beautiful painting. A home. Stop and admire it like he does, always saying, "Do you see that? Isn't it astonishing? Just look at that!"

Don't make mistakes. He tries hard not to and doesn't accept imperfection. Having high standards is the key to success. Easier said than done.

Keep looking for the next thing. He always has his eye on how to expand his business into new areas and tackle what's coming next. He stays in the mix and gets inputs from many sources. Staying static and resting on your laurels is simply not an option.

Give back. The ultimate philanthropist, my dad not only donates to institutions to improve the world but also sponsors inner-city students to get better educations—and everything in between. Donating money, time, and expertise is an obligation, not a choice.

Be on time. Show up. Follow the schedule. Don't disrespect anyone else's limited time. Don't make anyone wait.

Knock on the walls. Don't take anything at face value. When walking through a potential home to buy, no matter how great it looks, always knock on the wall to see if it's solid. This applies to all areas of life.

Don't be afraid to say, "Let me think about that." You don't always have to answer someone or respond to a request immediately. Wait and think it through. Don't feel pressured.

Do things differently. Have a vision. See what others don't. And act on it.

Prioritize education. Work hard. Stay in school. Get graduate degrees. Help others stay in school. Stay competitive in the world.

Don't sweat the small stuff. When my stepmother runs late, which she does often, he just shrugs. "She makes me really happy. I can't worry about this stuff."

Only take calculated risks. You shouldn't start anything you believe might fail. Be certain about things before trying them. If they don't work out, fine, but don't go into them with hesitation.

Tell stories. My dad told the best bedtime stories about a character named Murtle the Turtle. Be creative. Delight your kids. Meet them where they are.

Be affectionate. A hug. A thumb war. A pat on the back. A kiss. Show your kids how much you love them even in the smallest ways.

Make time for each child. My dad used to take me on "adventures," just him and me, traveling to Washington, D.C., or Colonial Williamsburg when I was a kid. Even now, when he takes me out to lunch, just me, I feel so special. No matter how many kids you have, dedicated time helps each one shine.

Write. My dad doesn't love writing, but he knew that his story would help others, so he spent years working on his book, *What It Takes: Lessons in the Pursuit of Excellence.*

Just keep going. And no matter what happens, especially related to aging, he always says, "It's better than the alternative."

25

Facing Our Fears

I asked my little guy to open the drapes.

"What if there's a man hiding behind there? What if he's going to kill us? What if there are deadly fire ants that come to life and—"

"If there's a man behind there, we'll both be dead in two seconds anyway. Can we see if it's a nice day out first?"

"I can't."

"You're watching too much YouTube."

"Mom, being scared isn't from YouTube."

"Come on. Face your fears. You'll feel better for the rest of the day."

He timidly opened one side of the curtains and hopped back under the covers.

Facing your fears has been the theme of my summer.

My little guys went to a small sleepaway camp in Maine for two weeks. Interestingly, my son wasn't scared when he slept in the woods one night under a "structure" he and his friends constructed out of branches and garbage bags. A bedroom in the Hamptons, though? Watch out.

Their camp's visiting day was an interactive experience in which all parents and siblings were supposed to take part in the activities, including "water toys" that featured two-story wobbling slides, climbable icebergs, and a trampoline connected to a Tarzan-like rope swing. There was no getting out of it. My kids had talked about my going in the lake with them on every call home.

My daughter, it turns out, was *waiting* for me to go in so we could "do it together" and hadn't been in the water the whole time except for a mandatory swim test. She'd been quite specific in her instructions: Bring a bathing suit and a cover-up ("your Zara dress is too short, Mom; wear a long dress"), sandals, and a change of clothes.

We got ready along with her older sister in her cabin, which smelled *exactly* how my cabin smelled when I went to sleepaway camp in the 1980s. What *is* that smell? Rotted wood? We walked down to the lake, our towels over our arms, sandals flopping.

"That's where the life jackets are," my daughter said, when we got down to the waterfront.

"Oh, I don't need a life jacket."

"Mom, you *have* to wear one."

"I'm sure they're just for kids."

"Mom, come on. You have to."

I looked around and noticed a couple other parents with life jackets on.

Fine. I searched on the rack for a dry life jacket and grabbed a size large.

"Mom, that's too big."

"It's fine!"

My daughter walked over and lifted it up and down with both hands. "It's going to end up over your head!"

"It's perfect! Don't worry!"

Moments later, I was standing barefoot on the splinter-filled walkway straight out of *Peter Pan*. Like Wendy walking the plank, I followed the kids down to the water, fully aware that my backside was on display for the rest of the camp. I tried to cover my butt—not even my butt, the area where my butt and legs become undulating mounds, to which menopause had added about twenty pounds. Does that area even have a name?

I peered over the edge. *I can't f—ing do this,* I thought. But my daughter was also scared. Shouldn't I be showing her that we can face anything? I had to do this! For her! For all the kids!

Finally, I told her the truth: "I'm ridiculously scared."

"Me too," she said.

My little guy offered his hand. "Let's go together, Mom," he said.

I took a deep breath, bit my lip in anticipation, and, holding his hand, jumped in.

Three-two-one . . . SCREAM.

"It's so cold!!!!! Oh my God! It's so cold!"

I bobbed in the water, my life jacket under my nose just like my daughter had warned me. But I'd done it. I was in. The kids swam over to me.

"Now it's time for the slide, Mom!"

Wasn't this enough?

The slide was attached to what seemed to be a surfboard platform. I struggled to hoist myself from the water, flopping onto the platform like a seal. Then, with a little nudging from strangers, I started scaling the wall, awkwardly finding the next slippery rungs with my hands and feet, my legs shaking.

Right as I approached the top step, I froze. I was going to have to jump up a little to make it onto the platform. If I overshot it, I'd go hurtling down the slide face-first. If I fell back the other way, I'd knock down the ten campers climbing up behind me.

"Come on, Mom!"

I couldn't move.

"I can't do it."

Campers cheered me on. My little guy held out his hand to help, but I refused to take him down with me.

"Well, I'm going," my older daughter said, and went down the slide without me.

"Wait, me too!" my little guy said, preparing to slide after her.

I screamed, "Do *not* leave me up here!"

The fit, eighteen-year-old lifeguard perched on the ledge was no help. He just stared at me. Who was this middle-aged mom who couldn't even get to the top? I'd like to note that I was the only mom who even attempted this.

Finally, a kind camper suggested I shimmy to the right to find better footing. By then, my ex-husband and his gorgeous, young fiancée had arrived and were watching, too. Good lord. Quaking, I pushed up that extra bit to get to the top, my eyes closed, and . . . phew. I'd made it. But then, it was time to slide.

"Push her!" someone yelled.

"Noooo!"

My heart pounded.

Another deep breath. Another bit lip and . . .

"AHHHH!!"

I dug in my thighs and started down the slide, which, devoid of water, basically became a skin-burn machine, the sounds of my thighs squeaking down the plastic echoing across the lake. I could hear my ex and my kids laughing. Fabulous. I couldn't even get all the way down. My body came to a complete stop at the base, my feet hanging over the edge, instead of catapulting in like everyone else. I clung there, holding up the line of campers, my legs on fire.

"This is the worst moment of my entire life!" I screamed, before flopping into the water.

After, the entire side of my leg had "raft burn," raw to the touch. Of course, it wasn't over then. I had to follow the kids onto the trampoline, where they insisted I ride the Tarzan rope into the lake. I was too afraid to let go when hovering over the water, so I went catapulting *back* to the trampoline, and all the campers waiting in line had to duck and take cover.

My body and ego were bruised, but what my kids would remember was that I had done it, like I'd promised.

"I can't wait until we do this again next year," my daughter said, as we walked in our towels back to the cabin.

"Next year?!"

She laughed and took my hand.

The drapes are still half closed in my son's room. But we're getting there.

26

How It Feels to Be Jewish Right Now

OCTOBER 20, 2023

This is one of those times when life seems particularly bifurcated.

Israel is the first thing I think about when I wake up, like a beloved relative who's in the ICU. *I have to check in. What happened? Are they okay?*

In my direct messages on Instagram, I have notes from friends all over the world, including one I received last night from a past podcast guest. Her daughter's dance team is desperate to bring back a member's mom and sisters—who are *hostages*. Could I help? *Me?* I wish! Can *anyone*? I gave what advice I could to support her in the moment, but it just felt inadequate.

At the same time, daily life in New York is chugging along with quotidian concerns. What should I make the kids for breakfast? I'm out of conditioner. Did I update that brochure yet? It all feels insignificant: How can I possibly be on the living room floor making influencer book boxes when there are such heavy concerns to hold?

One of the main things I'm hearing is: *Don't stop. Find joy. Keep going. Double down on life's simple pleasures, accomplishments, and celebrations. Double down on your commitment to the Jewish community. Double down on family, on work—you must!*

So, I'm continuing to record podcasts but I'm supplementing the schedule with urgent discussions with thought leaders around the world. Recently, I spoke to bestselling Israeli author and past podcast guest Einat Nathan, who Zoomed with me from Tel Aviv. I uploaded it immediately to our YouTube channel, unedited.

Einat, a chic, famous Israeli woman, has been talking to kids from the kibbutzim post-attack. She shared how the moms would show her their WhatsApp groups for their kids' ballet or soccer and say things like, *Look: Only two girls from this group are still alive.* Then the moms would ask her: "How do we explain this to our daughters, that all their friends are dead?"

She spoke about the mom who jumped out of a third-floor window, their "high-tech" safe room broken into, to avoid being burned to death. She turned it into a fun game to convince her three kids to do it. Her eleven-year-old broke both his legs in the jump. And yet, they ran.

I compiled an article with tips for coping by Child Mind Institute founder and author of *The Scaffold Effect,* Dr. Harold Koplewicz. I shared a beautiful, heartfelt essay by Sarah Sassoon, writing from Jerusalem, on Facebook. Earlier in the week, I interviewed a New Yorker, Rabbi Diana Fersko, about what she's saying to her congregation and what she's seeing.

Her book, *We Need to Talk About Antisemitism*, seems particularly prescient. We're certainly talking about antisemitism now.

I saw an old friend yesterday morning, one of my college roommates. She was asking—as many are—why? She was surprised by the level of vitriol and unmitigated hate. I explained to her that this type of thing is exactly what Jews for centuries have been alert to and prepared for. We celebrate Passover and discuss how we had to flee to the desert in Egypt without enough time for our bread to bake, so we eat matzoh. In fifteenth-century Spain we hid our holidays and celebrations to outlast persecution and keep traditions alive. We study the Holocaust, trying to understand how six million Jews were exterminated not even 100 years ago.

Every year, the same story, the same message: We must be ready. We are rarely safe. We are a wandering tribe, throughout history so often expelled from our lands, our homes. We celebrate Hanukkah and repeat stories of the destruction of our Temple in Jerusalem, and how, despite these attacks on the ancient Jewish community's most sacred place, we somehow found enough oil to keep the Temple's eternal flame alight. Today we light candles for eight nights. To remember that we survived.

Our celebrations are rooted in pain, designed to keep us on high alert.

We know that when a bat swings through a synagogue's glass door, as happened to Rabbi Fersko's Village Temple on East Twelfth Street in Manhattan, it isn't an isolated event. It's Kristallnacht. When swastikas start appearing in New York as they did at the 2nd Avenue Deli, they aren't isolated acts of graffiti. They are the beginning. The alarm bells. *Take notice. Be ready.*

This hatred isn't new. But it is back in a more overt way after a long hiatus. *Why?* Does it even matter? Why is *any* religion or race or gender or sexuality discriminated against? The important question is: What do we do about it? What *now*? The fear for "your Jewish friends," as all the Instagram posts are calling us, whom you're supposed to "check in on" like we have a cold or something, is deeply rooted in thousands of years of history.

When I was learning about the Holocaust back in middle school, I remember asking my mom, "Why didn't the Jewish people in Europe leave when things started getting bad? It seemed so obvious what was coming! Why didn't they go to different countries where they could be safe?"

My mom answered, "Oh honey. Because those were their *homes.*"

So? I thought.

As I look around my own home, my place of safety, security, and refuge, I hear that refrain in my head playing over and over. *Those were their homes.* When is it time? Where is it safe? Is it coming? Or will things proceed as normal, the way they have been? Six months ago, I was in Amsterdam, walking around Anne Frank's attic hiding space with my family, thinking: *Can you even imagine?* I can.

I want to scream: *You don't have to check in on us. You have to start asking yourself: To what length would you go to stand with us? To save us? If you had had Jewish friends back then, as antisemitism tore through Europe, would you have helped hide us? Helped us secure passports? Turned us in? What would you do if it all happened again? What* will *you do?*

It may sound alarmist, but this is steeped in the generational trauma of every single Jewish person, seared into our DNA like those tattooed numbers, imprinted on all our souls. It's why the chants "From the River to the Sea" and "Globalize the Intifada" are clarion call alarms to us. You might not be able to tell who we are just by looking at us. But make no mistake: We are a tribe. And we are trembling. Watching. Planning. Praying. What will happen next?

27

Yes, I'm Taking a Weight-Loss Drug

For the past couple of months, I've been holding something close to the vest. It isn't because I wanted to be secretive. It's because I didn't want to jinx it. But now, I'm ready to open up, like a new can of tennis balls. Whoosh.

Hello, Mounjaro.

Several months ago, I went in for a checkup that I'd neglected to schedule for two years. I'm the first person to tell someone else to see a doctor, but I was just too *busy*. There was too much going on. There was no time! I told myself.

Oh, please. I carved out an hour a day to grow my Instagram account. I couldn't pop in for a quick pap? But anyway. There I was, finally.

And I was *heavy*. That's what my late grandmother would call it when I'd "put on weight." Gagy would give me one of her warm, enveloping hugs, her chunky necklace hitting my collarbone, the smell of Trident gum emanating from her leather pocketbook. Then she'd pull back, take my face in both of her hands, smile at me with her giant, red-lipstick face under her beauty-parlor-set gray curls, and say, "Let me see you." She'd look me up and down, then say something like, "You look heavy, dear heart."

Turned out, I'd gained thirty pounds since the start of the pandemic. It was the perfect storm of lockdown, loss, menopause, aging, sleep deprivation, stress, and the slamming on the brakes of my lifelong workout habit. Nothing fit. Nothing. Not even my shoes. Gagy would not have been pleased.

At the doctor's office, the nurse asked me to step on the scale.

"Don't tell me," I said, walking over. "Is it okay if I get on backward?" I couldn't even face the number.

My doctor, at the end of our session, said in a very kind but matter-of-fact tone, "What are you going to do for weight loss?"

My eyes welled up with tears.

"I don't know," I said. "I've tried everything. My weight just keeps going up and up, no matter what I do."

Two years earlier, I had tried Metformin. No change. Then a year ago, I tried Ozempic. Ozempic made me so sick, I literally thought I was dying. I went away with some girlfriends to Miami, which I'd been looking forward to for months. But I couldn't leave the hotel room. The dear friend I was sharing a room with moved out. I couldn't stop vomiting and more, around the clock. It was *terrible.*

When I emailed *that* doctor, he was fairly blasé about it. It happens. Should be better in three-to-four days. Days? Every *hour* was terrible.

What about *nonmedical* intervention? he asked.

Yes, Doctor, that's what I've been doing since I was nine years old. And back then, I was *not* overweight. Apparently, I told my mother I was ashamed of my thighs, and, given the diet culture of the 1980s, she immediately whipped out the calories and carbohydrates guide and had me write down and calculate everything I ate. *One-quarter cup of orange juice.* Then she started taking me with her to Gilda's aerobics. I remember the night I swallowed my first pill, I had also met my goal of 1,200 calories and couldn't decide which achievement to tell my mom about first.

My summer at sleepaway camp at age eight was when I learned to stress-eat. I was so miserable that the only time of day I looked forward to was when the warm cookies came out.

"Okay, here's what we're going to do," my doctor said. "You need to see an endocrinologist who specializes in women's health."

Ugh. Great. Another doctor.

But I went. I had no choice. It was a medical issue. My cholesterol levels were high. My sugar levels were off. Everything was out of whack.

At the next doctor's visit, the endocrinologist looked at my bloodwork and listened intently to what I was saying. I recited the details of my weight history—yo-yo dieting, severe restriction in my late twenties and early thirties, all of it.

"You know," she said, "you're prediabetic, so your weight is going to keep going up. It's not about willpower or anything you're doing wrong. It's your blood and your relationship to insulin plus menopause. We need to do something to help you."

I almost hugged her.

She recommended Mounjaro. Few side effects. Super effective.

"You'll lose thirty pounds by the summer," she said, typing into her computer.

I laughed, disbelieving.

"You honestly think I can do that?" She looked me dead in the eye.

"Yes, or I wouldn't be a good doctor."

I went home, told *no one*, and filled the prescriptions.

I've had minimal side effects. The injection is easy, like an EpiPen. I basically just lost my appetite. Unlike Ozempic, which made everything taste bad to me, Mounjaro allowed me to enjoy food but stop eating before I was full. I could take a bite of a delicious chocolate-chip cookie—and then stop. Just stop. I didn't want it anymore. I was *satisfied* with only some of it. Ha! Do other people live like this naturally? No wonder weight wasn't an issue for them.

It was like a fantasy. The insurmountable challenge of managing my weight became a no biggie. In the first five weeks, I lost twelve pounds. All my clothes fit again. Dresses I hadn't worn in two years zipped right up.

I wasn't hungry. I stopped eating breakfast, not on purpose but because I was satisfied with my cup of coffee and didn't even think about it. In fact, I didn't think about food. Like, *at all.* I stopped snacking. My portions were small. I never went back for seconds. A big meal was two pieces of salmon sushi, a roll, and some rice. I wouldn't eat for the rest of the day. And I ate slowly. All without trying. It just happened.

When I asked the doctor if I needed a meal plan, she said, "Your issue isn't not knowing what to eat. You don't need a nutritionist. Just eat whatever. You're going to lose weight no matter what."

My weight seems to be stabilizing where I am now, but hopefully it'll stay on the downward trajectory. I'd like to get back to my pre-pandemic weight. Not my pre-baby weight or my Weight Watchers goal weight circa 2004. That ship has sailed. But I would like to reduce my cholesterol, get rid of the prediabetes diagnosis, and stay at a manageable weight for the rest of my life. Not svelte. Just comfortable.

Mounjaro is a miracle. I just hope I didn't jinx it.

(Note: I lost thirty pounds by the summer, exactly as the doctor predicted, with all my blood levels normal. Life-changing.)

28

The Anxiety Cheat Sheet

I never realized other people *didn't* have anxiety, because I've had it for as long as I can remember. Seriously, am I the only one who books multiple flights so I always have a backup plan?

Lately, I've been worrying about my kids. I mean, I'm always worrying about them, but my younger daughter left for sleep-away camp recently. I just know it isn't going well. I can feel it in my gut. The worst part is that I can't speak to her except for the ten-minute appointed calls after a full week has gone by. What the heck!? Isn't the whole no-communication thing a bit archaic in an age where we typically text each other fifty-seven times a day? Three phone calls a summer as if they're in prison? It would relieve all of our anxiety—parents and kids—if we could just simply *be in touch.*

Meanwhile, nowhere in the world feels safe. There are natural disasters, crime, and violence seemingly everywhere. So where is it safe to . . . *be*? The neighborhood ice cream shop

Rori's Creamery, four blocks away from my bookstore on Montana Avenue in Santa Monica, was recently robbed, windows smashed. Why do I keep thinking LA is safer than NY? I'm evaluating a zillion places. I even contacted a Zillow broker in Iowa.

To add insult to injury, a very mean person tore me to shreds recently in a particularly vicious way online—just because I'm Jewish and support the right of Israel to exist. I'm still reeling from this attack, even though I know I should "just ignore it" like everything else. But it was so hateful and *so* personal. It happened months ago, yet I'm still cautious about everything I do and say, the mocking voice in my head. I'm so tired of watching every sentence so carefully. How can people really connect without authenticity?

It feels impossible to keep my anxiety at bay, especially when the worries are actually justifiable. And yet, I have to try. Here's what I turn to when I feel myself spiraling.

Music. I remember during my third C-section (ten-plus years ago), I had my playlist going in the operating room and was like, "Why didn't I do this before?" Playing music calms me down and helps my system regulate. Yesterday I listened to the whole *How to Train Your Dragon* soundtrack. Don't judge. It helped.

Deep breaths. Ah, the old standby. But as I'm taking deep breaths, I'm trying to relax my body, releasing the stress I didn't know I was physically holding, starting with my shoulders.

Reading. I've read three books in the last couple of days, including *Awake* by Jen Hatmaker, which I devoured. I keep my head down and in a book whenever possible.

Spending time with my kids. I smother them. I admit it.

Writing. It always helps.

Making travel plans. Then debating changing them.

Doing cognitive behavioral exercises. I download worksheets for myself. I try to replace my thoughts in order to have a positive effect on my emotions. For example, pick a situation, like: My kid goes to sleepaway camp. My thought: My child is miserable! My emotion: terror, sadness, anxiety. My behavior: frantically contacting counselors, refreshing apps, crying, texting friends. Instead, same situation: My kid goes to sleepaway camp. My thought: My child is thriving! My emotion: happiness, peace. My behavior: back to normal! So, I try to plot triggers out and change the thoughts that influence my emotions and behaviors. It works.

Work. Throwing myself into my work every day helps take my mind off things. Picking books for my podcast. Editing copy. Interviewing authors. Planning events. Posting. All of it.

Social plans. Planning something to look forward to with friends, even just one lunch that will likely get canceled.

Gratitude and noticing nature. Being grateful for the birds chirping, the flowers blooming, my dog, Nya, curled up by my feet, the beauty of the sky and trees, the field of lavender I drove by, the feel of sand between my toes, the echoes of the ocean crashing on the shore. The sound of sprinklers. A light breeze on a warm day. Ripples.

Chocolate in any form. Hot, dark, chips, sorbet, cake, anything. I'm in.

And if all this fails, know that anxiety makes for some great writing.

29

Why Writing Matters

I gasped. No, the airplane wasn't going down. I'd just thought of a twist for the novel I'd been working on. It hadn't been part of my first draft. It wasn't part of the original outline. But it tied everything together perfectly. I couldn't believe it. I thought authors were joking when they said that eventually their characters start writing their own stories. That moment is why I love writing fiction.

My next novel, *Overheard,* didn't come together as magically. I wrote the whole thing twice. The first time, I was deep in post–October 7 accidental activism. My characters kept finding themselves in the middle of protests. My plot twists weren't believable. Every time I thought about the project, I'd groan. I wasn't having any fun writing it—and the reader would be able to tell. I was too embarrassed to even show my agent. After almost two years, I canceled my contract and gave back my advance. That hurt.

I thought about the hundreds of authors I'd interviewed and remembered all their fabulous advice to *keep going, keep writing, get in the document, let the magic happen.*

But writing is a leap of faith. It's banking on creativity, which isn't linear and doesn't adhere to, say, deadlines. For something interesting to happen in my novels, I know I need to have my fingers on the keys. Why write another novel? Why write at all? There is no lack of options out there. More books come out each week than anyone can possibly read. Do I really *need* to add my own story to the mix? What's it all for?

I write to achieve the same goal I've set for my entire company: to improve people's lives. To help. To make people think and feel. To connect people. To make people feel like they're a part of something. That they aren't alone in this big, crazy world. That their innermost thoughts and feelings are validated.

My goal is to connect people because those connections make people happier. It's to entertain readers while they're reading, yes, but also to find books that stick with them *afterward* and help them see the world in a better way. It's the same reason why friendship itself is important. A book is the greatest friend there is.

Do I do all this because I haven't always felt included myself? Perhaps. Is it because of all the times I've cried, like those first few weeks of college, alone in my dorm room, before I'd found my people, too embarrassed to walk across campus by myself to get dinner, so I stayed in and ate dry cereal instead? Maybe.

Perhaps I want to spare people from the emotion that has been the hardest for me to bear at different points in my life:

loneliness. That ache wraps me up like a scratchy blanket I can't shake off. The pain I'd feel walking down the street on a beautiful day in New York City when I was single, seeing all those other people eating at outdoor tables, laughing, when I didn't have any plans that night . . . or seeing groups of moms with strollers when I was pushing mine alone . . . or even now, seeing groups of people on Instagram out at fun parties or taking girls' trips that I wasn't invited to. Not that I could've gone. But it would've been nice to be included.

Maybe that's why I do it all. Because I deeply understand how it feels to feel *excluded* and so I've dedicated my life to helping others feel *included.* I host parties and dinners and retreats to gather nice people who are kind to each other. To help others get through hard times.

And this is a hard time in the world. Uncertain. Unsettling. Devastating.

I know deep down that every story matters in the same way that a coffee date with a friend matters. It's when we let our humanity slip out. When we understand and empathize and hug and smile. I could listen to people tell stories all day. Some days, I do.

Every book or essay is important because the sum total of all we've read makes us who we are. Ultimately, none of us *are* really alone, no matter how lonely we may feel, even if we're loneliest surrounded by others. We're in it together. And we can come together by just picking up a book, article, or essay. Or by writing one.

This morning, I got a message from someone I've never met about an article I'd written that came out earlier this week.

"I just wanted to thank you for your article. . . . You so perfectly articulated every fear I have . . . and it made me feel seen and less alone. Thank you."

To which I responded: "This is literally why I write!"

It's not always easy. Sometimes I get nervous putting it all out there. Things don't always land. But sometimes the comments have reassured me and surprised me. Moved me to tears. Fortified my resolve.

Writing is what I do. I let people into the darkest, most shameful, humorous, honest places and find, instead of censure, appreciation. Recognition.

We don't have too many places to share as we get older. Our marriages hide behind closed doors. There is no school cafeteria to sit in every day and confess. We are busy, trying to hold up so much, including the facade that it is easy or that we know what we're doing.

We don't know what we're doing.

None of us have navigated all the milestones from grief to passion to fear to aging—until we do. We need each other more than we think and more than we let on.

Sometimes I literally nod or say, "Me too!" out loud like a lunatic as I read what others confess. And then I turn the page before firing up my laptop.

That feeling. That magic. It's intoxicating.

30

I Am Not Lowering My Voice

I sat on my couch and sank further into despair and frustration. It had been another bad news day in Israel. I'd been speaking out about antisemitism and my support of Israel as a diaspora Jew since October 7, but nothing seemed to have an impact. What else could I *do*?

I'd never planned to be "publicly Jewish," as many now describe those of us who use our platforms to advocate for fellow Jews. I mean, I'd never *hidden* that I was Jewish. It just wasn't the most salient part of my personality, nor was it overly relevant to the mainstream conversations I was having on social media, on my podcast, or in my newsletters about books.

I was raised Reform in New York, had my bat mitzvah at Temple Emanu-El, got married at Central Synagogue, and helped Kyle convert to Judaism at Temple Israel. I lit Shabbat candles, when I remembered. I oversaw the Zoom b'nei mitzvah of my twins and countless family worship services.

Sometimes I'd post about Judaism when the spirit moved me: A beautiful Passover table. Our family's Hanukkah festivities.

I made the main character in my debut novel, *Blank,* Jewish, because of course I did. *Write what you know.* It wasn't even a conscious decision to make Pippa Jewish; she just *was.* I included a lockdown scene at a temple and gave the Hebrew school teacher a big role because Pippa's son was preparing for his bar mitzvah. I even named the teacher's dog Dayenu because: funny!

But I was always deeply proud and intellectually observant. At Yale, I researched children of Holocaust survivors for my class on Jewish identity. I delved deep into Holocaust books and movies, reading countless accounts of what happened. I studied. I listened. I learned. I knew I would be ready if the time came again.

And it did.

On the morning of October 8, I was in Denver at a regional bookseller conference for my publishing house. As I came out of the bathroom, my husband held out the phone and said, "Honey. There was an attack on Israel."

"There's always an attack on Israel," I said, taking a look.

"No, this is different."

My first instinct was fear. My dad had a trip scheduled to Israel that week. He'd just helped rebuild a library there and was going for the opening. Had he left yet? Was he there? Was he okay? I called right away, and, fortunately, he had been scheduled to leave two days later.

Back in New York, I talked to Anne, my business partner. Of course we would post on social media about it, both me personally and also on the company's social accounts. We drafted what we believed was a thoughtful and appropriate post; it read: "Zibby Media is devastated by the attacks on Israel. Our hearts go out to the victims and their families."

And that's when the wheels started to come off.

In the weeks and months that followed, I began to realize it as chants of "From the River to the Sea" rang out, especially in New York and on college campuses. For my own support of Israel, my name was added to lists of Jewish authors not to support. I got attacked on social media. Trolled on Goodreads. Some authors scheduled to appear on the podcast canceled. Several bookstores said they would boycott books that our company published—even when the authors were not themselves Jewish or expressed political viewpoints different from my own.

"Can't someone else's mom speak out?" my younger daughter asked during a talk at the dinner table.

Yes, I was scared to speak out. I'm *still* scared. I was scared that asserting my Jewishness publicly would get me in trouble. And it did. But I knew I had to speak up. What would happen if I didn't? What if *no one* spoke up? I had a platform that I had to use. If I could, I must.

Not only had I gotten so much hate, but I'd also gotten so much love. Jews and non-Jewish friends and strangers from around the world emailed, DM'd, and reached out to me at events. At every stop on my book tour for my novel *Blank*, at least one woman would approach me. Timid. Quiet. She would wait until the signing line had ended and come over to me, nervously, and then whisper, "I just wanted to thank you for speaking out . . . for all you're doing . . . for the Jewish people."

I'd hear about her cousins or friends or colleagues who had been in Israel on October 7 or who had been lost. I'd hear about the antisemitic attacks in her neighborhood. How she hadn't been sleeping. How all she could do was worry about her kids. Shell-shocked, the woman would reiterate how much it meant to have another voice out there: my voice. How it kept her from feeling alone.

"Thank you," she would say again. "Keep speaking out. We need you."

As I slipped my Sharpies back into my tote bag, collected my belongings, and thanked the bookstore owner or event host, all I could do was think about her.

What else could I *do*?

Around that time, I had become part of a group chat of thirty or so Jewish authors who came together as a community in conversation. It was like an online support group, out of which grew Artists Against Antisemitism, a 501(c)(3) founded by Alison Hammer after October 7.

By that summer, I was depleted. Discouraged. Nothing I said or did affected the tsunami of hatred. Why did I bother? For what? It wasn't making a difference. Nothing was helping.

Then, I had an idea. What if I asked the writers I knew and Jewish thought leaders I admired to write personal essays for an anthology about our experiences? I could start with the members of the group chat. I'd edited and published two anthologies already. I knew how to do it.

I wrote to the group: "Guys, I have an idea. What if we do an anthology of essays about our experiences. We'll donate profits to Artists Against Antisemitism!" They enthusiastically said yes and volunteered to help. We invited more than two hundred authors and activists to contribute essays, pro bono, to the collection within a few short weeks. Seventy-four accepted. Many others would have written had it not been for the tight deadline, they said, but I was determined to get the ebook, at least, out by October 1 to commemorate the anniversary of the attacks.

As I received each essay, I'd stop what I was doing to read it. Edit it. Send the revised essays off in batches to be copyedited. With every press of the keyboard as I worked on the manuscript, I was healing my soul. The staccato typing sounds were evidence that yes, there *was* something I could do: I could do *this*.

Reading the essays, I cried. I laughed. I took comfort in the stories and shared experiences and hoped others would feel the same way.

Editing what became *On Being Jewish Now* was one of the most meaningful endeavors of my entire career. It was a lifeline. We met our goal to publish the ebook and audiobook on October 1 and hosted an amazing day-long panel event with many contributors and an audience of New Yorkers. Just being together in that room on October 1 felt DNA-fortifying. The paperback arrived in bookstores on November 1 and, through several printings, spent twenty-nine weeks on the *USA Today* bestseller list. Readers were hungry, desperate to see themselves reflected. Later, it was adapted for the stage by The Braid and performed all over California.

Through the book, I've gotten to know Jews everywhere: Brazil, Australia, the UK. On Zoom, over email, on the phone.

When Jewish peers in Amsterdam recounted the night of the sports attack and Australian writers shared their grief and fear when their temples were burning, I felt the common threads deeply. And I published their stories on Substack.

I've seen firsthand that no matter where in the world we are, Jews are connected. We're a family. A community. I didn't feel that before. Now, it has a physical element to it. And there's something to being in person, to showing up, to congregating. It's a preservation instinct, to glom together like a beehive or a school of fish. It's an animalistic, evolutionary imperative that has taken over and that draws us to events. We get in our cars and drive, not really knowing why, so we can feel the comfort and security of being understood.

My mom recently told me a story from when I was a little girl. We were at a restaurant, Sweet Basil, and she and a close friend were talking nonstop. When the conversation moved to something related to Judaism, their voices suddenly dropped.

I piped up and asked, "How come whenever you talk about Jewish things, you always lower your voice?"

The two of them exchanged a look.

My mother replied, "You're absolutely right. There's no reason for us to lower our voices. Thanks for pointing that out." She told this story when accepting a Jewish advocacy prize of her own decades ago.

I am not lowering my voice. Join me.

31

The Palisades Fire

Two days after

The most destructive fire in LA history started just feet away from our home in the Pacific Palisades. Life has been a living nightmare since we first saw footage of the fire on our Nest camera, the flames dancing devilishly in our backyard. We've gone through every emotion as we've waited for news from friends, watching footage, trying to find information, mourning the loss of the life we were leading.

So many of our friends have now lost their homes.

"Any updates?"

"It's gone."

"Nothing left."

"We lost it."

"We lost everything."

How is this possible? I was just there! Everything was fine!

Kyle and I are still waiting for a complete update about our home. The firefighters heroically put out flames in our shed and the hedges. But then the flames came back and we lost service. Late last night, we found a video online from a man on a motorbike zipping through our neighborhood and caught a quick glimpse of our property. The house appears to still be standing, at least from the front. We don't know the full extent of it yet.

But it isn't about our house. It's about our life.

Our feelings. Our community. Our memories. Our beloved stores, restaurants, streets, sidewalks, neighbors. It's about the homes where we sat at friends' kitchen tables and played Uno, celebrated their birthdays, and truly connected.

It's all gone.

Even though Kyle and I both technically live full-time in New York, we spend a lot of time in the Palisades. I think Kyle might spend more time in LA than he does in New York. His company and my bookstore are out there. We created a beautiful, idyllic life that sustained us and gave us something to look forward to, always counting down until we could go back the next time.

In March 2016, Kyle and I were visiting Santa Monica for one of our first trips out west together. I was newly divorced, and Kyle and I were still in the butterfly days. I'd lived in LA (West Hollywood) for two years after graduating college, but he'd never been. My brother and his wife and kids lived there, so I wanted to visit.

While we were there, I took a photo that I thought would make a great gift for a loved one. I searched on my phone for a local photo-printing store; I wanted to print and frame the image. The closest photo store was in the Pacific Palisades. I'd heard of the Palisades and knew a few people who lived there but I had never been. Kyle and I drove our rental car there and promptly fell in love with the most beautiful hidden gem of a town, seemingly frozen in time. The little village was quaint, small, and filled with mom-and-pop shops. A local toy store. A stationery boutique. A frozen yogurt "shoppe" with a 1950s vibe. We wandered around the town as we waited the one hour for our photo print to be ready, ending up at Sweet Rose for ice cream. We were like, "What is this place?"

It felt like we were in an episode of *The Wonder Years*, in a place where the streets were safe, the families seemed beautiful and wholesome, and the scenery was lush, framed by rolling hills that were dotted by homes. As a jaded New Yorker, I thought, *Wait, do people really live like this?* It seemed . . . perfect. Was this an option?

Kyle and I started visiting LA anytime the kids were with my ex. I reconnected with old friends and spent days with family. We made new friends. Kyle and I began to think, *Could we potentially live there one day?* Of course, the travel itself seemed crazy, but once we got to LA, we relaxed, explored, and let ourselves grow into our new relationship.

We fell deeper in love with the city and each other on every trip.

We started popping into some open houses, one of my favorite pastimes. Where would we live in this new, pretend life of ours? We looked all over. We looked so much that we decided to work with a real estate broker, Melanie, who, it turned out, was from the Palisades and was happy to show us lots of places there. Just for fun, though. Right?

After some disappointing open houses, we caught sight of

another sign and decided to follow it to the top of a windy hill in the Palisades, wondering what was even up there. We parked, walked in, and gasped. We barely even registered what the interior of the house looked like; we were immediately drawn to the backyard. *That view!* From our perch on top of the quiet road dotted with 1950s-style one-story homes, one right next to the other, many seemingly trapped in a time warp, we beheld the most magnificent view ever. Mountains on the left. The city in the center. The ocean on the right.

Whoa.

Kyle and I looked at each other, jaws dropped.

By October, we had signed the contract on our new home—and had found a new friend in Melanie, who was one of the thousands who later lost her home in the fire. She showed us the ropes of the neighborhood once we moved in and introduced us to everyone we needed to know, especially as we renovated the place.

After close to a decade, we made that house a home. We hosted book events, cocktail parties, dinners at long tables under string lights, and even hosted a close friend's wedding. We got to know all our neighbors. Any time I walked in the house, I forgot about the stress of life in New York, the long flight, everything. I instantly decompressed. We filled it with books, framed family photos, and so many memories.

Our kids came out for every vacation, playing games in the pool and jumping on the trampoline. As we settled in, the new Palisades Village opened, bringing an upscale luxury mall right to our neighborhood. We alternated dinners there at the Draycott, Hank's, and later Angelini, with the "old" village.

Beach Street. The Yogurt Shoppe. Café Vida. The "new" village even had a bookstore! How great to have a bookstore in our neighborhood. But then it suddenly closed.

Sitting outside by the pool one lazy Sunday, Kyle said, "Hey, now's your chance to open that bookstore you always dreamed of."

"Very funny."

"Why don't you look into it? See if the lease is available."

I was scrolling on my phone anyway, so why not? I called the broker, who laughed me off the phone. No, no. They weren't looking for another bookstore there. (It became an Yves Saint Laurent.) I hung up. Case closed. But then the broker called back—and kept calling.

"I know you wanted something in the Palisades," he said, "but I have an owner who would *love* a bookstore on Montana." Montana Avenue was the main strip of cute shops and restaurants in Santa Monica, a fifteen-minute drive from our home.

"No, thanks," I said repeatedly. "It's too far away."

But after a few months, I considered doing a pop-up and went to look at the space.

It was perfect, a former dry cleaner I knew I could renovate to perfection. I had a vision.

Four months later, Zibby's Bookshop opened on Montana. It made perfect sense: In my dream life at my home tucked away on top of the hill, I could own my dream bookstore. Of course, I could. Because none of it felt real. Anything was possible.

The whole setup was idyllic. Safe. Spectacular. It felt too good to be true.

Apparently, it was.

"Honey, there's a fire! We're going to lose our house!"

Kyle was in Jersey City with his business partner Ethan. They were at a work meeting for the movie they were about to film called *Late Fame,* so we FaceTimed. He looked terrified.

"I can see the flames!" he said, looking at his phone, hysterical.

"What? Wait, screen-share," I said. "I have to see."

We watched as firemen raced back and forth. What were they doing? We could only see slivers, and not in the direction they were looking. How close was the fire? It was only later that a neighbor sent us a photo of what had burned.

The fire had spread everywhere. Three football fields a minute. We tried to figure out what was going on. By 8:30 p.m., Kyle got an alert from the security company saying that our indoor sprinkler system and fire alarm had gone off. By 9:30 p.m., another sprinkler alert. Then, one more: a heat sensor at our front door.

Then nothing. We thought we'd lost it.

We'd find out soon enough.

I saw video footage of our beloved village. The yogurt shop and Beach Street? Gone. Paliskates, our kids' favorite store? Gone. Gelson's grocery store, where we just recently picked up the *New York Post* and groceries for the break? Gone. The Starbucks where Kyle took my daughter while I was sick? Gone. The football field at Pali High, where we did the turkey trot over Thanksgiving? Gone. The rec center, where we played live ball, watched baseball games and soccer practice, and bandaged my younger daughter's hand after too many monkey bars? Gone.

It is an unspeakable loss.

At first, I was running on adrenaline. I felt the cold chill and sick bellyache that came with the intense fear of seeing the flames—and then I went into action, adrenaline mode. I would do anything I could. I posted our videos. When ABC News asked if I'd come on to discuss it, I said yes. Was it about me? No. But I wanted to put a face, a name, and an emotion to this tragedy.

"How great you weren't there!" people say.

But I wish I had been. Being away feels like I'm not a part of it. And my heart and soul are aching across the country as I sit alone in my office and try to make sense of the devastation. As I replay the footage and try to process images of the alphabet streets, gone.

Am I allowed to be this upset? Am I allowed to cancel work because I'm so distracted and distraught in New York? It seems ridiculous. But I can't focus enough to even read, let alone prep for podcasts. One minute, I'm crying on the floor of my closet. The next, I'm reaching out to friends and trying to put on a happy face to my colleagues. Am I just being overly dramatic? After all, I have my "real" home here in New York. Shouldn't I just suck it up and get back to work?

But how? My soul feels crushed. I know I need to jump in and find tactical ways to hclp. But first I havc to gct off the ground myself.

(Later, I would organize and run a clothing drive giving those that had lost their homes new, beautiful clothes from more than 50 brands. Later, I would give away books from the bookstore to anyone who needed them. Later, I would raise all the funds to replace the collections of four school libraries that had burned to the ground. But I didn't know that then.)

All I know is, I'm not ready for optimism and talk like "We'll rebuild!" I don't want to discuss home repair or construction. It misses the point. I'm still too shocked to think about recovery. I'm still uncovering the devastation.

Even if my home, or "structure," as newscasters call it, happens to be mostly okay, I've still lost something I loved more than anything.

We've all lost it. And maybe that's enough to keep the community together.

Eight months after

I sat in the driveway and cried. I couldn't do it.

This was supposed to be the weekend that Kyle and I moved back into our home in the Palisades after the fire. As it turned out, firefighters had arrived on the scene at our home early on, saving it. Apparently, our neighborhood was their first call of the day. They used our garden hoses to put out the fire that had raced along our property line, surrounding our shed on one side and scorching our plants, hedges, pergola, and outdoor furniture on the other. They put it all out and saved our home and all our immediate neighbors' homes, but then the flames had come back. It was just fate that saved *those* from engulfing our home.

Over the past few weeks, our contractor, Joe, and his team of workers finalized most of the repairs: replacing our burned balcony with a new blue-and-white tile floor, stripping and refinishing the table and pergola in the backyard, resuscitating the singed garage doors. Our AV guy, Maks, had carefully snaked new wires underground to replace those that had melted. Our gardener had removed all the old plants and grass—everything outside had been decimated. His team had planted fresh sod, sprinkling new dirt in the now empty flower beds.

The carpets on which piles of ash had drifted down through the cracks in our skylights had been steamed. Our beds were made with our "old" linens.

Kyle went there early to oversee everything. I'd been too upset to spend time at the house since the fire. The three times I'd gone had made me feel like I was in an alternate universe, our home suddenly plunked down in what looked like a war zone. Even the air inside didn't smell right. Nothing felt right. But I was confident that by now, September, eight months after the fire, it would be okay. Why shouldn't we move back? We missed it desperately. It was time. It—and I—would be ready.

And yet, I wasn't.

Midafternoon, I found myself alone in my car, driving up through the Palisades. As I rounded the corner on Sunset heading west, I gasped. Dozens of American flags greeted me at the start of the Palisades, where the National Guard had set up shop. Everything had been cleared into rectangular piles of packed dirt, all merging into one, making it look like open fields as far as the eye could see instead of hundreds of homes. Construction signs were the only markers separating the plots of land. I kept driving, my eyes filled with tears.

It somehow looked and felt like the Wild West, as if no one had ever lived there, as if the land was just now being inhabited. It was so big, so vast. And yet, I was looking at homes and belongings lost forever.

Unlike the first time I drove through town after the fire, when residents stood shocked in hazmat suits sorting through the rubble of what had been their homes, this time I knew many people had moved on. Families had filed permits to rebuild. Friends had sold their plots.

Relocated. Rented. Bought elsewhere. And yet, the destruction, the scale of it, was so massive that it still tore right into me.

Kyle and I used to walk up and down our hill often. It was a workout and one of our favorite pastimes. We would wander past the homes, many of them unchanged for decades, wondering who lived where, what their lives were like. We popped into open houses. We visited friends. We lingered. Noticed. We took in the sight of masses of lavender flowers at one house, the tinkling sound of fountains at another. We watched some houses be built over the years we'd lived there.

I cried most of the way up the hill. I gasped and covered my heart. Kyle was waiting for me outside with a big smile, but right away he could tell I wasn't okay. It felt like our home was in the middle of a graveyard. What? Were we supposed to make an espresso and relax looking out over all that devastation? The silence was chilling. I went inside. It looked the same but it . . . wasn't.

We sat on the couch in front of my desk where I did all my podcasts and looked out the window. The view was of the houses that remained and the many that hadn't, all the way to the ocean.

"It's just not time," Kyle said, understanding. "It's okay. It was just premature."

It felt like I'd lost the home all over again. Did I even belong in LA anymore? If only I could just live at my bookstore.

"What if we try again?" he suggested. "Maybe it'll feel better tomorrow. We'll go up, have coffee and watch the sunrise like we used to."

I was skeptical. How could it be better? But why not? That ping of optimism slid into my soul again. *What if?*

"We'll go up the other way this time," Kyle said, meaning we'd enter our neighborhood from the west side of Sunset. I hadn't gone through that part of the neighborhood.

We stopped at the Starbucks in the Highlands area of the Palisades at 6 a.m., looking at the WELCOME BACK sign and then, with coffee in hand, drove up the street, where we saw the first home we toured during an open house, where we met Melanie, where our dreams of an LA life first became reality. House after house had a story. House after house was gone. I looked over and Kyle had tears in his eyes, too.

"It's really bad over here," I said, taking his hand.

The sun still hadn't risen when we pulled into our driveway. We parked in front of the closed garage door in the dark and looked at each other.

"I can't even go in," I whispered.

"Let's leave," he said. "It's too soon."

And then he backed out and we headed downhill in the dark.

I miss the giant green mountains to our left, where hikers wandered, small specks in the massive trees and boulders. I miss the sounds of kids swimming, of music playing, of cars zooming, of dogs barking. What is a neighborhood without its people? I miss being a part of something. I miss being in the house, yes, but also being outside, waving to walkers heading uphill. I miss our life there.

I know—I was so, so lucky to have had it at all. But I am still mourning what we lost. I worry about so many things to prepare myself for bad outcomes. This was one I couldn't have prepared for. It was so big, I forgot to worry.

There are so many people from the Palisades who are displaced. Yes, they settled elsewhere, but that doesn't mean they've found new homes. How could they? Streets don't become well traveled overnight. Patterns must be established, shortcuts and rituals memorized. What is our world without a familiar container? It feels disorienting.

Most of the time when people move, it's a choice, a well-planned decision. People move for a *reason*. But this was no one's choice. The reason was senseless. Horrific. It's hard to process. It's hard to move on. And I don't want to move on. I want to go back. But I can't. And even if I could, there's nothing I could have done to prevent what happened.

On our way back down the hill in the dark, we drove along a few streets we hadn't visited yet. As we turned onto one, we were stopped in our tracks by a massive tree that had fallen in the middle of the street.

"Holy—"

Kyle slammed on the brakes. I just stared at it.

Uprooted.

Exposed.

Like all of us.

One year after

I'm sitting on my favorite couch in the world in our home in the Palisades. The sun hasn't come out yet, so all I can see are the twinkling lights of the city below us. I didn't think I'd ever get back here. So many neighbors and friends weren't as blessed. But finally, after a year, here I am. Changed, like the landscape around me. But here.

I will never feel truly safe again. It was an illusion anyway.

As it turned out, the fire was arson. It was *intentional. Someone* did that. Evil knows no bounds.

Miraculously, the barren mountains are now covered in a green so bright it looks like they're in a Disney movie. It doesn't even look real. And it's December. I don't remember them ever being this green before. It's like a shag carpet draped over all the hills.

The town and surrounding area have been cleared. No more beams. No more piles of rubble. No more army corps standing sentry at the entrance to our neighborhood.

Wooden frames dot the landscape. Some stores are open in the village.

Lights are on in the apartments on Sunset. Holiday decorations twinkle in front yards. It isn't the same, of course. It never will be. But there is life. There is joy. There is hope.

I drove up the hill almost exactly one year after the fire to move back in.

My phone was connected to my car, and I accidentally pushed a button on Apple Music that shuffled all my songs and played tunes I hadn't even realized I'd downloaded. A song from *The Greatest Showman* called "From Now On" blasted over the speakers.

I turned up the volume to hear Hugh Jackman singing about coming home again.

Goose bumps. The universe at work. We were coming home.

We slept in the house last night for the first time in exactly a year. I brushed my teeth at my bathroom sink as if nothing had happened and yet so much had happened, so much had been lost. I climbed into bed—our same sheets! our same mattress!—and looked down at the lights surrounded by verdant hills.

The natural world is stronger than I could've ever imagined. It survived the devastation and came back even more beautiful. Plants. Trees. Grass. Hills. It all grew back. Not the same. But better. I appreciate it all so much more now. Crazy to think of tiny me, standing on the edge of it all, doubting the land months ago, to now, with it all blasting to perfection.

I'm on my couch writing, our first morning back. The sun is finally peeking over the hills. The ocean glimmering in its morning slumber. The breeze yesterday had my hackles up. Could the wind cause another fire as bad as the last one? Are we safe? No. None of us are really *ever* safe. And yet we rest on the land and pray and hope that we're given a little more time in the beauty of the universe, that the rage doesn't come for us directly, so we can marvel in the magic of the moment.

We are changed.

But we are home again.

32

Signed Copies: My Journey to Authors Night

When I was a stay-at-home mom longing to become a published author, I used to attend the East Hampton Library's Authors Night religiously, sometimes with one of the kids in my arms, other times on a rare sojourn out during bath time and bedtime. I'd zip from table to table, a stack of books in my arms signed by authors I couldn't *believe* I'd met. So many authors in one place was a dream come true. I'd leave, my arms straining with the weight of overstuffed book totes, knowing I'd soon be lost in a new collection of stories once the kids were asleep. But deep down, I longed to be on the other side of the table. Would I ever get there?

I set up shop interviewing authors at Authors Night in 2018. It was thrilling. I carted my giant microphone and laptop out and interviewed Florence Fabricant of *The New York Times* and designer Ellie Cullman. I was behind the scenes! The room where it happened, as . . . press.

In 2019, I came back as a sponsor with my own booth, which, the night before, new friend and favorite author Dani Shapiro helped me decorate with posters of all the previous podcast guests. I dashed to the East Hampton copy center moments before Authors Night began to make posterboard printouts for the tent, which flapped and fell over in the wind. Treats and Nene came and worked behind the booth. Treats posed for a photo with Alec Baldwin, giddy from meeting him.

By Authors Night 2020, which was canceled, Treats and Nene had passed away from Covid.

Cut to 2022. The world and our family had been through trauma. Along the way, my book publishing dreams had come true. I'd had multiple books come out including my latest, *Bookends: A Memoir of Love, Loss, and Literature.* There I was, stepping behind the table, wearing a name tag that said AUTHOR. The thrill of it! It was even better than I'd hoped. I was the one signing books! Yes, it hurt that most people smiled politely and walked right by my table, on their way to the famous authors instead, but I understood. At least I was in it. On the other side.

In 2024, I came back for my debut novel, *Blank.* I'd arrived after a Slim Aarons–themed birthday celebration, so I was channeling my 1970s era. Stacks of *Blank* were piled up on my table. Would people take one? I celebrated every "sale," but wondered: Should I try to become a movie star just so I could sell more books? That would really speed things up. But at least I had a steady stream of visitors, unlike my first time.

In 2025, I showcased *On Being Jewish Now.* I was seemingly

more in demand than ever. An NPR reporter did an interview with me in one of the press stations. A camera filmed me at my booth. I had officially moved from press to author. I couldn't see the path in the early days, but over the past decade, I'd gotten there.

I wish I could go back and tell the stressed-out mom version of me that one day, her dreams would come true. But who knows? Maybe she already knew deep down that they would—or could. Maybe that's why she never gave up, which was the message of my children's book *Princess Charming.*

Meeting new crops of authors annually under the tent gives us all the confidence to keep going, like they did. One line at a time. Those authors aren't just writers. They are goal-seeking, resilient dreamers who had just enough confidence in their work to keep going. I am honored to be one of them. Maybe next year, you will be, too.

33

Missing Howard

It's morning in Arizona and I'm in the kitchen where my stepfather, Howard, should be—always was—and he's not here. I woke up early to my mom sitting alone, having coffee—and I burst into tears. Not that Howard would've been up this early, but his mug is empty by the coffee maker, his phone and watch on the counter. He's not coming back.

I open the fridge to get milk for my coffee, and the plate my mom always has ready for him for breakfast, a Saran Wrapped melon and berries ready to go or a bagel or muffin, aren't there either.

It's dark out and all I can hear is my own crying.

My throat is raw from sobbing so much. It's embarrassing. I can't seem to control it. My mom isn't a big crier, nor is my daughter. The three of us hug in the dark as the Keurig spouts. I apologize for the drama as I cry, knowing, of course, this is not about me. I'm supposed to be there for my mom. I don't mean to be selfish. But I can't stop. It floods me.

I'm typing on the kitchen counter now and his reading glasses are right here, the thick black cord still wrapped around them. How will he never wear them again? How is this possible? The words on the screen blur as my eyes fill again. I need to get a handle on this.

Yesterday on the plane to Arizona with my daughter, I went through every picture of "Howie" on my phone—the "search by name" found 1,167 pictures, which I then uploaded to a shared family album. I went through each one and texted the best shots to the people he was with. Holding my younger son as a baby. Making silly selfie faces with my younger daughter, their tongues out, their eyes crossed, laughing. Playing baseball in the backyard with my older son when he was three. Having a serious conversation with my older daughter, age six, and her doll.

There were hundreds of him and my mom. In the early mornings reading the paper. Decked out in black tie at night. Always in sync. And so many family photos of all of us. Gosh, he was everywhere. He didn't miss a single moment for any grandchild. Every play, every graduation, every important and not-so-important moment, he was there. Smiling.

"Hey, kid," he'd say. Always followed by a compliment.

My mom and Howard mostly live in Arizona now. They sold their New York apartment this year, which we collectively said goodbye to; a group photo captured us in front of the boxes. They spent summers in the Hamptons. Howard basically lived at the golf club. Someone called my mom yesterday to tell her the flag flying in front of the stately clubhouse was now flying at half-mast for Howard. It was one of the times she lost it.

My mom and Howard had moved back to Arizona for the season the day before. We'd all just said goodbye to them in New York. They'd come to our home for Rosh Hashanah and break-fast. The last thing I said to Howard as we hugged was "Be safe," always worried they'd get into a plane crash or a car accident. You never know. But it didn't occur to me that they would arrive in Arizona, and he would be gone the next day, after ten minutes of feeling dizzy, from a pulmonary embolism. I'm grateful there was no pain.

When my mom called to tell me, I answered from the student center of my son's school where we'd just arrived for his Family Weekend. I couldn't hear anything so assumed she'd accidentally called me, which had been happening often. But then she called again a few minutes later, hysterical, and, it turns out, from the hospital.

I slid on the floor and sobbed. I won't go into the ugliness of my reaction, Kyle and me together, wailing. I stayed on the phone with my mom as she left the hospital, on speakerphone as she unlocked the car and slid in, holding his clothes. She didn't want to leave him alone. We booked flights immediately. My brother came in from LA and was there within hours, thank goodness.

Everything felt like walking through sludge. I kept saying, "My brain isn't working right now." I know that's what happens to me during grief, a typical response, where only about 10 percent of my executive function works and basic tasks seem impossible. I slept in my clothes and wore the same thing the next day—until I got to my mom.

Somehow, I'm going to get through this because we all get through everything. But this is different. Howard is part of my immediate family. My phone's home screen is a photo we took late last summer, laughing. Howard, my mom, Kyle, the kids, and me on the staircase.

I know he's not my "blood" relative and I'm incredibly close to my own "real" dad, too, but for anyone who doesn't have a step-anything, it doesn't matter one bit. It's love. Love doesn't need a DNA test. Howard's two daughters are the ones more entitled to be sad. His grandsons. His "real" family. So I defer to them. But he is as real to me as anyone, with my mom every moment, a constant, soothing, delightful presence for thirty years. God, we were so lucky. How is that chapter over?

I'm feeling the pain for all the things we won't get to do with Howard. The graduations. The dinners. How he was always there, no matter how late, to pick us up from the airport. The quiet moments at home.

Howard should be sitting in his favorite chair, TV on, as I write this. But the chair is upright. Empty. My mom is puttering around, hyperfunctional as usual. And I am doing what I know helps me. Writing.

34

FanWing Fest

My younger son coerced me into reading the first installment of Tui T. Sutherland's *Wings of Fire* series. I was prepping for an upcoming podcast when he took *my* book out of my hands, tossed it onto the floor, and replaced it with Book One of the series.

"Mom, it's so good. You should read it."

"Honey, I have so much to do—"

"Forget your work. You'll love it."

"I really don't have time—"

"Mom, you read like a thousand books. Just read this one book. I really think you'll like it."

Okay, fine. This was how he wanted to connect. Wasn't *that* worth more than anything? Message received.

"I'll do it," I said.

"Yesssss!"

For the next few days as I made my way through the novel, my son would repeatedly ask, "What part are you up to now?"

It was my first fantasy novel. Despite the ubiquity of the genre, I had never really been into the idea of reading about dragons. Getting into the narrative had been a challenge. Wait, which dragon was Clay? What did it mean that Tsunami was a SeaWing? How many wings even were there?! I couldn't keep it all straight, consulting the map and introductory descriptions often. But by the end, I was hooked. I *cared* about those dragons.

"I can't believe they put all of them in cages! So not fair," I said as I put my son to bed.

"Right?"

Even my daughter got into it. The three of us had dinner table conversations about the various characters, professing loyalty to one tribe or another, and debating which character the next book in the series should be about.

When Tui's next book was announced, I excitedly rushed over to show the kids the new cover. I'd never felt cooler than when a brand asked me to collab on their plush *Wings of Fire* characters for the holidays. Turns out the way to the kids' hearts was through the land of Pyrrhia.

When I saw on Instagram that Tui was participating in an event called FanWing Fest, I knew I had to take the kids. To Atlanta. When sales opened, I was ready to pounce, convinced it would sell out in two seconds. I muted a Zoom meeting and quickly snagged seats online. Yes! The kids were going to freak out! I'd later find out that the event hadn't sold out, ever.

With plushies in hand, books in backpacks, wings at the

ready, we flew down to Atlanta after school for the event. I booked us all a room at what I thought would be a nice hotel, but when we arrived late Friday night, it was in full-on party mode. Picture club goers in tight outfits, giant earrings, and bright lips streaming by us as we checked in.

Police were stationed all over the lobby.

"Is everything okay?" I asked the closest cop.

"Yep, just Friday night here," he said, chuckling.

Ah.

We ordered room service and locked the door.

The next morning, the kids were as giddy as if it were their birthdays. We were out the door at the crack of dawn, only to line up with hundreds of other families outside the church that was hosting the event. Finally, we got into the church and found . . . more lines. Lines to get into the rec room, where six activities including face painting were stationed. Then, lines at each station. Lines for the bookshop pop-up. Lines for the bathroom. Lines for the food trucks. But we were at FanWing Fest!

The kids bounced around, posing with various characters and getting books and plushies, as I followed them like their personal press corps. The best was meeting Tui.

"Wait, I know you," she said. I had been stalking her on Instagram, explaining how obsessed my younger kids were.

Embarrassed, the kids hid their faces as I told her about the podcast she and I had done together years earlier with my older son. I also mentioned that the kids and my mother had lined up and waited in her signing line at the Tucson Festival of Books, which I'd posted about afterward. My God, was I being creepy?! I even took a photo with Tui *without* the kids. Wasn't the whole point to impress *them*!?

By the time the day wound down, we were filled with memories and exclusive fun facts Tui had revealed during her speech. Sometimes, as I'm scrolling through my Photos app, an image from FanWing Fest will pop up and I'll smile. It was all worth it.

After I read my younger son a few other parts of this book, he said, "You should write about FanWing Fest."

"You're right!" I said. "I should! Great idea."

That's why I stopped my other work today: so I could record the times that mattered instead of focusing on the tasks that don't. Whatever my son suggests next, I'm in. Turns out he's the one teaching me.

We have our copies preordered for the next book in the series. We're counting down. And Tui? Please don't block me.

(Note: As I edited this essay, my email dinged with a notification: The next FanWing Fest dates were just released. We are so there.)

35

Here in the Middle

I never thought TikTok would bring my family closer together, but it did.

One of the kids saw a clip of the TV show *The Middle* months ago and asked if they could watch it on an actual TV. I was delighted; usually I have to *beg* them to put down their iPads, saying, "Come on, just move your eyes to a *different* screen. . . ." But I turned it on and then sat down on the couch to see what the show was all about.

I *fell in love.*

Since that first episode, we've binged it as a family, our post-dinner ritual. I've quoted the show eight million times. I've thought about it endlessly, usually long after the TV goes dark. I bring it up whenever possible. I've googled the stars. I even tried to find a map of their fictitious (I checked) hometown of Orson, Indiana.

When I found out my daughter's orthodontist was from

Indiana, I was like, "Wait, have you watched *The Middle*?" I was dying to talk to someone about it. She loved it. We bonded over the Frugal Hoosier grocery store.

It has helped me more times than I'd like to admit. I feel like Frankie, Mike, Axl, Sue, and Brick are doppelgängers of my own family in a way. When the Colts—their team—are on TV, we're all like, "Go, Colts!"

Technically, the show is about a family of five confronting the challenges of the everyday. Each season follows a school year and takes us through everything the kids experience, from homework issues, team tryouts, and dance invites to driver's license attempts, injuries, and college acceptances. Basically, life.

But it also follows the parents' issues. Frankie starts out as a car saleswoman and transitions to being a dental hygienist. Mike works at the quarry. They bicker, drink beer, and wonder if they're lazy parents. They struggle financially. One of them recently said, "We've cut so many corners, we're a circle at this point." The kids fight. Frankie gets upset at being made fun of. She schedules office hours to try to get a handle on the onslaught of kid requests that make her brain feel like a sieve.

So why do I love it so much? I love it because it's the most authentic depiction of parenting and relationships I've ever seen—and because it shows life in a family from everyone's perspectives. It's really a show for each of us individually.

I love Frankie's voice-overs, which always kick off each episode with "Here in the middle . . ." When we watch as a family, we all get a better understanding of what we're each going through. The short, expertly written episodes, usually only twenty-one minutes, pack a huge punch. They make us laugh at the Heck family, yes, but also at ourselves.

My life in some ways couldn't be more different from theirs. A few seasons ago, the Hecks won a trip to New York (well, really Sue did) and the dad, Mike, had never even been on a plane. Yet here I am, watching the show from our New York apartment, traveling constantly.

We all like to think our experiences are unique. But "here in the middle" we realize that's not quite right. The arguments. The stresses. All of it. They're universal. I used to look forward to my late-night snack, counting down to time alone in the kitchen once the kids went to bed. *The Middle* has replaced that habit as my end-of-the-day decompression. I crave it.

So many of us are "in the middle" these days. Issues with kids. Issues with parents. Issues with marriage. All of it, all at once. *The Middle* celebrates quotidian concerns and elevates banter into art. We can all complain about what's on our very full plates or we can join Frankie and Mike in the car at a drive-through, grab a seat next to Brick in his folding beach chair at the dinner table, listen to Axl torment Sue, and laugh.

The episode when Axl graduates from high school and the next one when he goes away to college had me crying for hours. Literally. Sobbing. The kids were like, "Mom! It isn't real." Was I crying because Frankie was or because I knew a few months from now that would be me with my twins heading off to college? That it would all be over soon? Both.

I'm already counting down to the next episode. But I'm not ready for it to end. Any of it.

36

Bittersweet Gratitude

I'm waking up to a quiet house pre-Thanksgiving with sleeping children, the morning sun stretching over the lawn, a fresh cup of steaming coffee, and a book I can't put down. Is there anything better?

And yet, yesterday, driving home from Starbucks with my older daughter in the front seat, I clicked on my right turn signal to pop by and visit my mom and Howard and realized Howard will never be there again. I started crying. Sudden loss doesn't feel any better just because someone was in their eighties.

I've realized that there *is* no emotional preparation for missing someone. There is no preparation for pain. I try. I anticipate. I worry in advance. But the future absence of someone is something the mind can't fool itself into being ready for. When it happens, it just hurts, like a knife hurled in through the top of my head that slices through to my toes.

Sometimes the pain passes as fast as it comes. By the time I pulled into my driveway, I'd wiped my eyes and carried in the Starbucks Refreshers, a smile on my face. But it often lingers, heavy on my chest. (Don't even get me started on how toxic Refreshers are. I can't believe I used to allow my kids to drink them.)

Today, my house is full. Footballs will fly. Cheers, echo. We'll laugh like we did lying in a heap together watching *The Middle.* I know it is all fleeting. I'm trying hard to clutch it to my chest by taking photos, writing, paying attention, begging my mind to record every detail. But no matter what I do, these moments and memories will also pass.

Last night in the middle of dinner, my younger daughter said, out of nowhere, "One day, I'll be the grandmother and I'll be telling everyone about you!"

Slayed.

She later whispered, seriously, as if I could control it, "Please don't get Alzheimer's."

We are all aware of it, the ticktick of time, and the people we can't be with on a day supposedly about family. It is imperfect, this Thanksgiving celebration. But I am still thankful.

I'm thankful for the abundance I've been given in my life so I can give back and help others. I'm thankful for the unlikely, magical outcome of having four children, a great second marriage, a fantastic family, and wonderful friends. I'm thankful for everyone I can still hug and for the memories of everyone I wish so much I could hug today. I'm thankful I got to love them at all.

My mother frequently uses the word "bittersweet." I think it fits.

37

College Admissions

I'm stretched out on the couch, scrolling Instagram, waiting for the rest of the kids to come in to watch *The Middle*. Kyle is in the armchair, my younger daughter on the other couch, the TV paused. Out of the corner of my eye, I see my older daughter enter holding an envelope, perhaps the one I'd stashed behind the rest of the mail earlier in the week, yet another college mailing I'd almost thrown away.

"I think I got in."

I glance over. She had just finished her applications. While she'd applied early decision to her top choice, which meant she'd have to enroll if they accepted her, she'd applied rolling admission to several others. Those decisions could come in anytime and weren't binding. I knew she'd added a few schools at the last minute, but I didn't recall the name on the envelope.

"No, honey," I say. "You didn't apply there."

She starts reading.

"Congratulations, you have been accepted . . ."

What?!

I swing my legs off the couch and leap up. Kyle and my younger daughter also walk over to her.

"Wait, *did* you apply there?" I ask.

"We are pleased to offer you a scholarship. . . ." she reads.

"What school even is this?!" Kyle asks.

"Yes, I applied, Mom. Remember? This is just the abbreviation," she says, pointing to the letters on the folder.

Oh, right.

"Did I get in?" she asks. "I did, right?"

"Let me see."

None of us can believe it. We all huddle around to look at the letter. How could the decision have come back so quickly? But it did.

"Honey! You got in! You're going to college!"

"I'm going to college!"

"She's going to college!"

"I almost threw that away!"

We are all screaming. My son races in, too. The five of us jump up and down together, cheering.

"She's going to college! She's going to college!"

Until we got the letter, college had been theoretical. We'd been holding our breath knowing that both she and her twin brother would eventually get in and go *somewhere.* But the black ink, the bold font, the scholarship, made it real. She was going to college. But who still sent paper notifications in the *mail*?

Knowing she had one acceptance made the wait for her first-choice notification more tolerable. When that college's email came in, she wasn't home, so she called me on FaceTime while her friend videoed her.

"I GOT IN!"

"AHHHHHHHH!!!!!"

I screamed and screamed.

My son also had good luck. I waited for his decision in the back seat of my car in the dark before heading into a speaking event. FaceTime again: his dad in one square, me in another. As the seconds ticked on, I started sweating, bit my lip, and nervously rubbed my hands together. Come on!

And then, "YESSSSS!"

He raised his fists triumphantly in the air.

"In!"

"AHHHHHHHHH!!!"

More screaming.

I still smile thinking about it.

After all that, they had gotten in. When we started looking at colleges, my daughter and I had driven six hours together, listening to Shaboozey's "A Bar Song (Tipsy)" repeatedly as we navigated the Northeast. We'd almost had our car stolen from a sketchy hotel when a man tried to steal our keys as we waited at the valet stand. We'd gone on school tours in blizzards and in 100-degree heat.

My son drove as we looked at schools. When we toured one university, I tripped on an uneven sidewalk and went flying; I fell with him holding me up by one arm. At another school, the tour was so long that I had to lie on the floor on my back, my legs up against the wall, to relieve the pressure. We'd eaten pizza out of the back of our car, laughed hysterically when I couldn't figure out how to put the pillows back properly on a pullout couch at a college inn, and spent countless hours debating next steps.

I started one of those childhood flashback montages. Calling around to different preschools at the appointed time in Manhattan to get applications. The mommy and me classes. The paper crowns for special days. Singing together at morning assembly. The first day of kindergarten. Pushing the double stroller across the park. Playdates. Mealtimes. The tears. The sports tryouts. The rejections that had me crying almost as hard as they were. The crushes, the heartbreaks, the repeated driving tests, the stress.

I'd been worried about the twins since before they were born, and now this was it. Adults. College.

A few minutes after my daughter got accepted to her first choice, I got a new text.

Do I need to fill out a form or something?

Okay, maybe they aren't totally independent just yet.

I remember my first day of college like it was yesterday: what I wore, who I met, the pit in my stomach as my parents and brother left me in my tower room on campus. Would I be okay?

The twins have been gone from home a lot, so that feeling won't be entirely new, but gone for four years in new places? In *college*?

I think about all the mistakes I made in college, what I wish

I could do over. I'm tempted to give them reams of advice, but I know they won't listen; they'll have to forge their own paths, make their own mistakes.

Also, how can I be old enough to have kids going to college? I still feel just as young now as when I went. And yet, they're turning nineteen, and I'm turning fifty. I was a young-ish mom for them, now an old-ish mom for my youngest, which he reminds me often. I don't *feel* almost fifty. Fifty sounds scary. But my dad is turning eighty next year and he says he still feels about forty. Perhaps we never really feel our ages. But the clock ticks anyway.

I'm so proud of the twins, but I'm scared. What if something *happens*? I can't protect them anymore. I have to trust that I've given them the tools they need to get through this crazy life. But did I?! *I'm* still finding my way.

I take a deep breath, like I did when my son first merged onto a highway with me gripping the passenger seat in abject fear, my eyes squeezed shut. There's no going back. We're on the ramp. Now, I'm the one along for the ride.

"Hey, Mom? We forgot about my friend's birthday party this weekend!"

"And I need help studying my vocab words!"

Cut the montage music. My younger son and daughter are trying to get my attention.

"Mom! Stop typing! Close your computer!"

"Wait one sec, guys. I have to finish this!"

My older daughter calls me on FaceTime. "Do you think it's too early to go to bed?"

Kyle texts me a photo of a package that was just delivered at our home in the Palisades, the flowers blooming as the sun hits the yard.

My mother forwards an email from a friend saying how much she loves our new Instagram series with a note: "Fabulous!"

My older son texts, We were undefeated this season!

Amazing! I text back, as my younger son calls for me again.

Amazing, I think.

A new chapter begins.

38

Travel Companion

I look over at the empty seat in the airport restaurant and feel an ache. I can feel my eyes welling up. I'm thinking about Kyle not being there, and I'm thinking about my mom missing Howard. Usually when I travel for work, Kyle comes with me. I always say, "You totally don't have to come. It's fine. I'll be fine!"

But if he can, he joins me.

"I hate to think about you traveling alone," he says.

Admittedly, I have a tendency to almost crash into things, especially other travelers. I have zero spatial awareness, and I'm pretty sure I'm starting to lose my hearing. Regardless, I just can't tell if a person is nearby. (I've googled it and I don't think it's a real disorder.) So when I'm traveling, I accidentally turn suddenly and whoops!

"I'm so sorry!"

I'm also (eek) on my phone a lot as I walk, so that makes

things even worse. I know. When I'm with Kyle, he often steers me to one side or another like I'm blindfolded. We usually laugh about it, but sometimes, when I'm sleep-deprived or extra-stressed, I snap.

"I don't need you steering me around like I'm a child!"

But, okay, fine. I kind of do.

Sometimes I tell Kyle not to travel with me because I secretly think I could be *even more productive* if I were alone. I could, perhaps, send *even more* emails. Read more pages. Write more words. Post more. Cross more things off my never-ending list. Like a pit bull, I will *not* let that task out of my teeth no matter how hard someone tries to pull it away. *I must finish.*

I've explained to Kyle that sometimes I feel like I'm a doctor in surgery. If a doctor was operating, would her husband feel like she could open that funny Instagram video right away? Of course not. Obviously what I do isn't a matter of life or death, like it often is for those in the esteemed medical field, but hopefully he gets what I mean.

I view every flight as my operating theater. I race against time, seeing how much I can do before arrival. Sometimes I'm *glad* there's no gate or that the jet bridge is malfunctioning, because I can squeeze out that much more of the task at hand.

"I'm almost finished," I say, way too often. "One sec."

And yet.

I miss him.

I miss sitting next to Kyle at the counter of whatever restaurant or coffee shop we wander into, seeing his smiling face. I miss seeing his luggage standing at attention next to mine. I miss our casual banter.

"Want to go in here?" Or, "Honey! A bookstore." Even, "Looks like we line up over there."

I'm particularly sensitive to this temporary absence because of my mother's new permanent one. Howard has been gone for three months now. I still can't quite believe it, his sudden death something my brain can't process. It still feels like he *must* be around somewhere. Isn't he, say, getting ready in the other room? Maybe over at the club hitting a few balls? Down at the post office talking to the guys? How can he be *gone*?

I was so worried about my mother at first. How would she cope? How could she come home to an empty house after thirty years with Howard? And yet, in part due to her obsession with her dog and constant companion Murphy (whom she calls my "brother") and her many, many friends, she seems to be doing okay. She's incredibly busy. She doesn't feel lonely because she quite enjoys being alone. Grief only hits her at certain moments.

At school pickup together the other week, my mom confessed to having one particularly vulnerable moment. Waiting a beat so she could collect herself and tell me without crying, she said, "The hardest time is right after a movie or a show ends, and I stand up to grab Howard's arm and he's not there. And I forget."

And then, suddenly, she's crying.

"I really want him to be there. But he's not. And he's not coming back."

I replay that scene on the sidewalk over and over again. Her face contorted with pain and shock. Our big hug as we stood amid unknowing parents and nannies chatting mindlessly as middle schoolers streamed through the double doors.

Kyle and I squabble like any other couple. We go through ups and downs, of course. But there's no one I'd rather be traveling through life with as my partner than him. Being with Kyle makes life funnier, more interesting, more fun. I laugh a lot. I get excited noticing things just so I can tell him the story. We hold hands. I ask his advice about everything: "Post this slide first or this one?"

I take another bite of my soggy cinnamon raisin bagel, the white craft paper wet with butter on the counter next to the to-go coffee. I can hear the conversation we would be having had Kyle joined me on this adventure. But we're not having it. He's off having important work meetings of his own, as he should be—and I wouldn't want it any other way.

But I miss him. And knowing how quickly things could change makes even his temporary absence press on my chest. Because *what if?* What if he suddenly disappeared like Howard and I could never do something as simple as sit at a counter for breakfast with him ever again?

So, I call him. We FaceTime, laughing as usual, catching up until it's time to head to my gate. Still holding the phone on FaceTime, I slide off the slippery stool, grab my suitcase handle, and turn to start walking—and almost crash right into an elderly gentleman.

"Oh my gosh, I'm so sorry!"

Kyle shakes his head on FaceTime.

"Honey! You said you were fine traveling without me!"

"I am," I say, laughing, as I merge into hallway traffic. "I promise. I am."

But I'm not.

39

Taxi Talk

"What should we call these little *repartees*? Taxi talk? Everyone can relate to being in a taxi."

"What? No, Mom. They can't. Not everyone has been in a taxi!"

"Well, most people have."

"No, they haven't."

My mother and I are in the back seat of a cab crossing Central Park on the way to pick up one of the kids. I'd started posting little scenes between us several months before, quotes from our everyday lives in dialogue bubbles on photos of us interacting. They've become the most popular thing I post. So much for starting a business and reading thousands of books. All I had to do to get more likes was post about my mother.

Recently, a woman approached her at Nordstrom.

"Are you Zibby's mom?"

"Yes, and you are—?"

"I follow Zibby on Instagram. Love your series with her!"

She couldn't believe it.

"Moi! Recognized in Nordstrom!" she'd said, beaming after her shopping expedition. "Can you *imagine*?"

It all started because I was taking pictures of her after Rosh Hashanah dinner and she snapped, "What do you even *do* with all these photos? You certainly don't post them."

I could tell she wanted a bit of spotlight shined her way. For years, she had given me framed photos of herself and Howard as holiday gifts. Okay, fine.

After the dinner, I sat on the couch, giggling, capturing the conversation we'd just had about our hair, our dresses, our outfits.

"What are you doing over there?" Kyle asked.

"Oh my gosh, I'm cracking myself up," I said. "I'm writing this scene with my mom. I don't know why. I just find it so funny. I'm going to post it."

Turns out, others found it funny, too.

In that first post, she'd mentioned that she didn't *love* her new haircut. The next morning, she called me from the salon chair.

"Well, turns out Susannah follows you on Instagram," she said. "She called me right away and told me to come back in so she could fix it. So here I am. Funny, right?"

Funny. Right.

But not always. I'd just posted our conversation about how she didn't want to pay for my newsletter subscription ("Why should I?") and eventually relented ("Fine, I'll do the cheaper one.").

"You know, Mom," I said, "your comments used to offend me."

She waved at the air and pursed her lips. "I know. I'm so glad you've matured a lot lately."

Of course.

Growing up, my mom and I fought constantly. As I became a mom myself, we battled over boundaries.

"But I'm their *grand*mother," she'd say. "I should be able to come and go as I please."

We're in a much better place now.

In fact, the series itself is bonding us even more.

"I wonder what our next *vignette* will be?" she says, a glint in her eye as she hugs me hello. "Just don't make me look stupid."

"I won't, Mom."

Since Howard died in October, our relationship has shifted. I've tried to be there for her as much as possible. I'm doing it for her, but also for him. Howard was always trying to mediate our squabbles, help us get along. I see his photos as they slide by on the digital frame next to our coffee maker.

"I'm trying, Howard," I say to his smiling face. "I'm doing my best to take care of her."

I can hear him saying, "Thanks, kid."

And so, the things I've become used to—her giving gifts that I don't necessarily want, like the faux-fur coat she bought herself, foisted on me as generosity—are now mined for comic relief.

There are two main types of comments on the posts. The first are from people who have lost their moms.

"I envy you," they say.

"She reminds me so much of my late mom."

"I wish I could have a moment like that with mine."

The second type are from people shocked to see their own families in mine.

"Omg, we have the same mom!"

"Are you in my brain?"

"Our moms must be twins!"

In sharing what I now find funny, most the time, in our everyday dialogue, I'm finding a deeper connection with others than even books can bring; it's that universal mother-daughter duet.

The conversations and posts have helped me, too. Now I can just give my mom a glance when she says something outrageous, and she'll crack up laughing. She hears herself the way I would write it and finds the humor.

And so we laugh.

Just like Howard wanted all along.

40

Short Stack

I'm sitting in the kitchen in front of a plate of pancakes. I'm about to rush out the door to get the kids to school and then head to my office, where I'll spend the morning preparing for my event with Rachel Goldberg-Polin about her new book, *When We See You Again.*

Soon I'll be sitting onstage with Rachel, connecting with her in the aftermath of losing her son, Hersh, who was taken hostage on October 7, 2023, held for 328 days, and then murdered by Hamas. Twelve hundred people will fill the synagogue as far back as I can see. I will reel from the conversation about life, loss, love, faith, motherhood, writing, and more, and won't be able to do almost anything else for days, steeped in the soulfulness of Rachel, stewing in sisterhood.

But now, before that happens, I'm looking down at my four perfectly stacked pancakes that Kyle has just cooked for me with love. He has even heated up the maple syrup. It has been almost ten years since we moved into this home together, engaged. I'd unpacked with kids on my hips, not knowing what would come next, not realizing my office upstairs would host thousands of podcast conversations, and my living room would bring so many readers and authors together.

I'm settling back in at home after my older daughter's admitted students weekend at her new college. I'm still chuckling at the updates my son is texting me from his. How can you *forget* a sleeping bag knowing you're sleeping on a buddy's floor? I feel like both kids are ready, in their own ways, for their next adventures—and I am *so* excited for them. Walking around my daughter's soon-to-be campus and learning about the offerings, I long to have the chance to do it all again knowing what I know now. But it's her turn.

I dip a delicious, fluffy bite into the warm maple syrup and "mmmm" in delight. Food will always bring me enormous pleasure. I flash back to being nine years old, already counting calories, and having my mother place one small pancake on my plate with a spatula, measuring out my one tablespoon of syrup. I see my dad turning around to show my brother and me how he can flip the pancakes high in the air and have them land perfectly back in the pan. I flash forward to lingering in New York diners with my high school girlfriends, rehashing the events of the night.

Where did I get my fix of pancakes in college? I can't remember. Then Denny's in Los Angeles with new colleagues who laugh about "Moons Over My Hammy." I move to my mid-twenties, when a boy and I stay up all night connecting over pancakes at Florent in the West Village, paving the way for several years together. I zoom ahead to the end of business school, clutching a broken rib as my ex and I hit IHOP. Then making chocolate-chip pancakes for my own kids as the sun rises. Finally, packing boxes of pancake mix in my "influencer boxes" for my novel *Blank,* sending them out to help with pre-pub buzz.

Now I'm devouring this perfect short stack as my middle schoolers plan "NeeDoh-hunting" trips after school, the latest craze, while I'm en route to my event. Mounjaro, of course, has helped me eat fewer confections at a time. There's nothing that could make me welcome back the incessant, punishing food noise that has finally vanished.

Earlier this week, I watched the start of Dan Senor's conversation with Rachel from the Temple Emanu-El Streicker Center, where I've moderated events for several years. As the broadcast started virtually on my laptop, my younger son asked for help with a complicated math study sheet. There was a puzzle we had to figure out: "What does the sea monster eat?" Each answer corresponded to letters in the solution. I took advanced calculus at Yale and could barely figure it out. By the end of it, after we'd both exploded in frustration several times, we gasped when we deciphered the code.

We got so excited that we jumped up and down, screaming the answer: "Fish and ships! Fish and ships!" I could hear Rachel speaking in the background and could feel her loss of Hersh, his spirit circling. I hugged my guy as tightly as possible. It was cruel and unfair that Rachel couldn't do the same anymore. So I would do it twice as hard.

Later tonight, I will walk through the synagogue to meet

Rachel. And I will feel in my cells that everything I've done until that point has led me right here, exactly where I am supposed to be, connecting onstage with one of the most amazing women in the world, channeling her wisdom, her Jewish values, her resilience. Rachel's fierce love for her son, Hersh, and the sacrifices she has made as a mother make her our hero. The power of her words. The strength of her stares. The boldness of her actions. Rachel puts into corporeal form what all of us know: There is nothing we wouldn't do for our children. She does it all with grace, class, soul, and an animalistic love that we all feel.

My mom will call me after watching the YouTube video. She will tear up.

"Zib, do you know how proud I am of you? *Really* proud? I know you've doubted sometimes just how much I love you. But I love you beyond words. Do you know that? I love you so much."

My dad had recently conveyed similar thoughts.

"I can't believe when people come up to me and say, 'You're Zibby's dad, right?'" He had laughed. "That's what I've become in my old age! Zibby's dad. Ho ho ho."

Maybe that's all I have been looking for all along. My parents' approval. Love. Acceptance. Praise. Attention. Validation. It's so basic, but so essential. I'm almost fifty and still seeking that powerful affirmation that somehow steels me for everything, including being a parent myself. Is there anything more fundamental to who we are as living beings than a parent's love? Sometimes I imagine life without my parents. Who would I tell? Who would I be? What would any of it matter if I couldn't hold up whatever I'd just accomplished like an eager child with a newly discovered seashell and say, "Look!" And yet, somehow I'm the mom, too, filling that role for my own kids. Am I doing a good enough job?

"Guys! Time for school! Let's go!"

We scamper to the door, backpacks on, laptops packed, the sweet taste of syrup on our tongues.

Soon Kyle will have three movies he produced out in theaters. Soon my brother, fresh from a Best Picture Academy Award nomination, will further expand his film business, becoming a full-on studio. Soon my two younger kids will have their bar and bat mitzvah. Soon I will take my two daughters and my mother on a Paris adventure. Soon my best friend Gen and I will take a trip to celebrate our fiftieth birthdays. Soon the twins will settle into college. Soon my dad will turn eighty after I turn fifty. The clock ticks.

Later this week, we will go out to dinner at an Israeli restaurant in New York: the four kids, my ex and his wife, Kyle and me. We will laugh, joke, talk over one another, show pictures on our phones, and have a great time as the rain pounds on the roof. It will have taken almost eleven years to get here. But we are here. My ex and his new wife have exciting things on the horizon, too. An important next chapter for all of us.

I say hello to other families waiting for the school bus downstairs. I am no longer shy; I'm the one welcoming in the wobbly.

We drive to school as I read the kids their horoscopes. What's in the stars for the future? I don't know what the next decade will bring. I never could've predicted this one. But I know that when crisis hits, I will be there to help. I will read hundreds more books. I'll text my kids a trillion times and spend time with family and close friends. I'll set up shop in my bookstore and meet many more wonderful people.

I'll get to know more authors and have meaningful conversations. I'll connect people who don't even know each other today. I'll advocate for the Jewish people, condemn antisemitism, and do what I can to protect our community. I'll keep writing and potentially publish more books. Perhaps that novel I never finished? I'll make many mistakes. I'll laugh about most of them. I'll experience shattering losses, lose people I love. I'll make new friends. Hopefully I'll witness the Palisades getting completely rebuilt. And I'll likely post on Instagram another 5,000 times. And I'll eat more pancakes.

That is, if I'm lucky. As Kyle reminds me frequently, "We *get* to do this." Until we don't. So off we go. Together. Arm-in-arm with loved ones, lost and living, and with each other. Pass the syrup.

Acknowledgments

Thank you so much for reading *Between Chapters*. I am truly grateful that you took the time out of your busy life to do so. What'd you think?! Email me at info@zibbyowens.com if you loved it. Share your *Between Chapters* stories at zibbyowens.com.

Thanks to my team at Zibby Media for slotting *Between Chapters* into the production schedule and not complaining, despite how many times I interrupted our other conversations to say, "What do you think about . . . ?"

A special thanks to Anne Messitte and Kathleen Harris for thinking it was a good idea and working tirelessly to get it done, Chelsea Grogan for all her production magic, Sherri Puzey for her marketing prowess and suggested edits, Graça Tito for helping with the cover design and line editing, Holly Mauskopf, Vanessa Vazquez, Liz Ziemska, Amy Brosey, and Rachel Kowal for reading drafts, and Jordan Blumetti for editorial help. Thanks to Lauren Kucerak and team for the publicity support. Really, thanks to the entire Zibby Media team: Gabriela Capasso, Sarah Fradkin, Sierra Grazia, Violet Guinness, Madeleine Letellier, Mary Marolla, Allison Pollack, Tessa Savage, Mike Rizio, and all our amazing booksellers! And thanks to the home team: Tenzin, Zompa, Dahlia, and Kevin.

Special thanks to the Z.I.P.s (Zibby's Important People) from Substack who read an early draft and provided helpful comments, especially Carol Orange, Diana Levy, Sarah J. Abitdol,

Kristi Kasper, Laura Brady, Renee Lonner, and Amy Sunshine. Thanks also to everyone who came on the Palm Beach Retreat and provided cover and title input. (Secret: the earlier titles were *Catching Up*, *Here in the Middle*, and *Between Books*.) Thanks to Annie, Elizabeth, Will, Alyson, Mary, Lucy, Ellen, Kyle, my kids, and my mom for additional—endless—cover feedback. Also thanks to everyone on Instagram who weighed in! There were at least one hundred and fifty other designs I dreamed up before waking up at 3 a.m. and taking the picture on the cover—and changing the title, again.

Thanks to Two Rivers/Ingram for distributing the book and to all the booksellers who decide to sell it. Thanks to my agent Joe Veltre for always rooting for me. And thanks to everyone in "the Zibby-verse" (haha) for being a part of it all.

Thanks to everyone who offered a blurb for the book (go back to the beginning to read those).

A huge thanks to my husband, Kyle; my parents; my brother, Teddy, and family; my friends; my extended family; and everyone referenced in the book. I love you all so much.

Thanks to all of you who have been on this wild ride with me, from watching it unfold on social media to chatting at pickup. I couldn't have done it without you.

Mostly, thank you to my four kids. Simply put, you are everything to me. Special thanks to my younger son for editorial help throughout the book.

My twins will have just headed to college as this book comes out (God willing). I might be a mess while navigating yet another life stage. But that's why I write. To soften the falls. To soothe the soul. And to sort it all out.

Thanks for going through it with me.

Source Attributions

Some of the essays were inspired by or adapted from the essays below.

"I Had to Lie to Find True Love," Zibby Owens, *Vogue*, © Condé Nast, 2/12/24

"How Reading Helped Me Through My Divorce," *Moms Don't Have Time to Write* on Medium, 2/3/21

"A Mother's Right to Sanity," originally published as "A Mother's Right to Sanity: Starting The Movement to Just Be a Mom and Not a Family Management Exec," HuffPost.com, 10/7/17

"Finding My Voice," originally published as "Finding My Voice: How Writing Turned My Childhood Shyness into a Gift (A Story for Kids and Grown-Ups)," *Moms Don't Have Time to Write* on Medium, 2/11/18

"Let's Lose Weight Later," originally published as "Hey Moms, Let's Lose Weight Later," HuffPost.com, 10/20/17

"Family Trips," originally published as "Pro Packing Tips from a Seasoned Traveler and Mom of 4," *Kveller*, 5/3/18

"At a Bat Mitzvah the Night of the Pittsburgh Shooting," originally published as "At a Bat Mitzvah the Night of the Pittsburgh Shooting, Celebration Mixed with Sorrow" *Kveller*, 10/28/18

"Journey Women," originally published as "A Love Letter to That Mom Friend You Don't Talk to Every Day," *Kveller*, 11/9/18

"Don't Crush My Butterflies," *Moms Don't Have Time To: A Quarantine Anthology* © 2021 by Cottage 8 Communications LLC

"I Risked My Life Getting to Curriculum Night on Time," *Moms Don't Have Time to Write* on Medium, 9/27/19

"My Boys," originally published as "Time Keeps On Slipping into the Future—Especially as a Mom," *Kveller*, 5/29/19

SOURCE ATTRIBUTIONS

"Our Own Memorial This Memorial Day," originally published on *Moms Don't Have Time to Write* on Medium, 5/31/21; also published on Thrive Global (www.thriveglobal.com), 5/31/21

"Why I 'Write' Anthologies," *Moms Don't Have Time to Write* on Medium, 8/29/21

"The Secrets of Divorce Pain," originally published as "Let's Name Divorce Pain" on Thrive Global (www.thriveglobal.com), 8/11/21; "Back on Meds: How Medication Lifted One Mom out of the Darkness," HuffPost.com, 4/29/14

"Don't Miss Your Connection," originally published as "Finding the Friends That Fit," *Moms Don't Have Time to Write* on Medium, 10/8/21

"Saving Time," originally published as "Online Holiday Shopping May Save Time, but What Do We Lose?," *Moms Don't Have Time to Write* on Medium, 11/15/21

"What's Your Sign?," *Zibby's Highlights* on Substack, 7/21/23

"*You've Got Mail*: Revisited Twenty-Five Years Later," *Chicken Soup for the Soul 30th Anniversary Edition* © 2023 by Chicken Soup for the Soul, LLC

"Getting Back on the Horse," *Zibby's Highlights* on Substack, 8/4/23

"My Mother's Napkin Holders Mean Summertime and Love," originally published as "My Mother's Napkin Holders Mean Hamptons Summertime (and Love)," *Dan's Papers*, 8/16/22

"Lessons from My Dad," originally published as "30 Things I've Learned from My Dad," *Moms Don't Have Time to Write* on Medium, 6/18/21

"Facing Our Fears," *Zibby's Highlights* on Substack, 8/18/23

"How It Feels to Be Jewish Right Now," *Zibby's Highlights* on Substack, 10/20/23

"Yes, I'm Taking a Weight-Loss Drug," *Zibby's Highlights* on Substack, 11/10/23

"The Anxiety Cheat Sheet," originally published as "The Top 3 Things I'm Worried About Today and the 11 Ways I Cope," *Zibby's Highlights* on Substack, 7/16/25

"Why Writing Matters," *Zibby's Highlights* on Substack, 6/28/24

"I Am Not Lowering My Voice," originally published as "Why We're All Here," *On Being Jewish Now: Reflections from Authors and Advocates* © 2024 by Zibby Media LLC

SOURCE ATTRIBUTIONS

"The Palisades Fire," originally published as "What I Felt Watching the Palisades Fire Threaten Our Home," Katie Couric Media, 1/10/25; "Uprooted," *Zibby's Highlights* on Substack, 9/15/25; "One Year Later, We're Back in Our Palisades Home" *Zibby's Highlights* on Substack, 12/30/25

"Signed Copies: My Journey to Authors Night," *Social Life Magazine*, June 2025

"Missing Howard," *Zibby's Highlights* on Substack, 10/12/25

"Here in the Middle," *Zibby's Highlights* on Substack, 1/16/26

"Bittersweet Gratitude," originally published as "This Might Help," *Zibby's Highlights* on Substack, 11/27/25

"Travel Companion," *Zibby's Highlights* on Substack, 1/21/26

About the Author

ZIBBY OWENS is the bestselling author and editor of six books, including *Blank*, *Bookends: A Memoir of Love, Loss, and Literature*, *Princess Charming*, and *On Being Jewish Now*, which has spent twenty-nine weeks on the *USA Today* bestseller list and inspired an accompanying essay platform and stage adaptation. She has contributed to *Vogue*, Oprah Daily, *Good Morning America*, and *The Washington Post*, and writes a bestselling weekly Substack. Owens hosts the award-winning podcast *Totally Booked with Zibby* and the weekly TV show *Totally Booked with Zibby* on JBS (Jewish Broadcasting Service).

A frequent speaker, moderator, and broadcast guest, Owens is known for highlighting the book industry's most anticipated new releases and emerging authors. In 2021 she founded Zibby Media with the launch of Zibby Publishing and unique year-round hosted retreats and events for book lovers. In 2023, she opened Zibby's Bookshop, the independent bookstore in Santa Monica, California.

A graduate of Yale University and Harvard Business School, Owens, a mother of four, lives in New York and LA with her husband. Find her online @zibbyowens and www.zibbyowens.com.